To Mimsi & Dirk,
In warmest
friendship ~
Love,
Carla

OTHER WORKS by
CARLA MARIA VERDINO-SÜLLWOLD

<u>Screenplay</u>
Raising Rufus: A Maine Love Story

<u>Books</u>
**We Need a Hero! Heldentenors from
Wagner's Time to the Present
A Critical History**

Top Cat: Tails of Mannahatta

Method & Madness
*Orpheus, Dionysus, and Apollo: Dialogues
with the Gods & Other Essays*
Singing in Solitude: Essays in the Arts

<u>Monographs</u>
*A Bridge Between the Generations: Peter
Hofmann's Rock*
*The Heldentenor in the Twentieth Century:
Refining a Rare Breed*
*I Am the World: Thomas Mann and Richard
Wagner: Two Early Novelle*
*Pirates in a Paper Sea: A Manifesto on Music
Criticism*

<u>Translation</u>
Peter Hofmann: Singing Is Like Flying by
Marieluise Müller
The Servant of Two Masters by Carlo Goldoni

<u>Internet Content</u>
Thomas Hampson: I Hear America Singing
www.pbs.org

Raising Rufus
A Maine Love Story

by

Carla Maria Verdino-Süllwold

Weiala Press
An Imprint of Mannahatta M.C.
Brunswick, ME

Raising Rufus: *A Maine Love Story*
© by Carla Maria Verdino-Süllwold
published by Weiala Press, an imprint of Mannahatta M.C.

Front cover, text photographs by author
Rear Cover photograph by Josette Bordiga

Library of Congress Control Number: 2011936801
Library of Congress Cataloging in Publication Data available

Verdino-Süllwold, Carla Maria, 1947 –

ISBN 978-1-4507-8463-4

PRINTED IN THE UNITED STATES OF AMERICA
FIRST EDITION 2011

To my dearest Gregs,
Forever Love

In Loving Memory of Gregory J. Süllwold
September 11, 1946-February 23, 2010

Acknowledgements

To my dear friends and best critics, **Albert H. Black, Jay Chandrasekhar, James Grace, Emily Lodine,** cousin **Donna Pucciani,** and **Mark Wright**, for their suggestions, encouragement, and support in the development of this manuscript and the screenplay version;

To **Malcolm Duffy** for his assistance with editing and proofreading;

And to **David Whiteside** for his counsel, support, and encouragement in helping me find a voice again.

Prelude

A ribbon of undulating cerulean divides sky and land. The opalescent sand sparkles under the caress of the morning sun. A spherical beacon, its buttery rays filter through the Maine morning fog, warming the waves, flashing a greeting to the pulsating Seguin Light.

As the white caps wander in and out, the tide slowly receding, the sandbar advances like a humpback whale, its pale, grey-pink iridescence stretching toward the horizon.

On the deserted beach, the languid water laps over the sands, smoothing them into a blank slate on which only emptiness is now written. But morning on the beach at Popham holds an air of eternal expectancy. On this brisk September day, the sea, the sky, and the sand wait for nothing in particular or for everything possible.

Chapter One

Twenty-five miles away, a blue van, bedecked with symbols of a busy life in the cities, speeds blithely toward its destination. For its passengers this September day is EVERYTHING. The van pulls off the Route One Connector in Topsham and crosses the iron bridge over the Androscoggin into Brunswick. The river rushes over the dam with primal fury.

In deference to speed limits, the blue Chrysler Voyager ambles more politely down wide Maine Street, past the small town shops and restaurants, the Gulf of Maine Books, past First Parish Church and the statue of Joshua Chamberlain, past the college of Bowdoin and down along to the fork where the road divides for Mere Point. At a pond flecked brightly by the morning sun, serenaded by duck chatter, the van signals a left and pulls into Meadowbrook. It winds through streets named for trees – Hemlock, Beech, Sumac, Alder, Tamarack – and chugs to a stop as the road turns to dirt.

The still youthful sixty-three-year-old couple climbs out of the van and stands back to take in the majesty of the hundred-foot pines. The trim sandy-haired man with strong Nordic features and riveting, robin's-egg-blue eyes inhales deeply. A thin smile twitches the corners of his bow-shaped lips. His dark-haired wife slips her arm through his and engages the eye of the ascending sun.

Their reverie is interrupted by the sound of a pickup truck grinding to a halt behind their car. They turn to greet their builder. Rob Ashland extends a hearty handshake and motions them to follow him. He has blueprints in hand and leads the way through the trees, indicating the fluttery orange ties that reprieve certain trees from the ax and pointing to the stakes that mark the footprint of the house.

Their tour complete, the trio returns to the vehicles. Another handshake and broad smiles seal the agreement. Rob waves cheerily and drives away.

Maria and Gösta Sundergaard linger a moment in the stillness, staring at the forest. Then, with the intuitive timing born of thirty-seven years of marriage, they impulsively throw their arms around each other and hug deliriously.

✳✳✳

Popham Beach wears its late afternoon insouciance. The pearly strand is ruled with the long violet shadows of sunset. The white caps roll in as a few gulls glide above the waters. In the distance, two dark cobalt specks penetrate the privacy of the place. Hand in hand, Gus and Maria stroll in silence.

Maria's voice, usually schooled and confident, sounds small and girlish as she breaks the stillness.

"How long do you think it will take to build it, Gus?"

"He promised us by May," her husband replies. "I'm sure he will. This is Maine, you know. Not New Jersey. People like to keep their word."

Maria nods. "Can you believe we're undertaking this at our age?"

"Well, we've learned a lot from our North Bergen house – what we do and don't want. It's exciting, really!"

"Yes, it is," Maria murmurs. She looks searchingly into Gus' eyes.

He replies to the unspoken query: "We've come a long way to get here, haven't we?"

"Thirty-seven years."

"That's not what I meant, Maria. I meant you and I – us – together."

"I know. It's been our dream." Maria stops and takes a step toward the ocean. She breathes in the salty air and makes a sweeping gesture toward the horizon. "Look at it! Oh, Gus, this is Paradise!"

Gus stands behind his wife and puts his hands on her shoulders. He does not speak. Together, they continue to stare at the sea, mesmerized by the liquid rhythm.

Finally, Gus leans over and whispers gently into Maria's ear. "It's a whole new life for us, a new beginning. I can't believe how damn lucky we are!"

Seized by an impulse, Maria bends down, picks up a small piece of driftwood, and traces onto the sand a heart shape. Inside it, she inscribes the words *12 Tamarack Drive*.

Gus smiles. He takes the stick from her and crouches to add his own inscription. Beneath their new address, he etches the date: *9/11/2007*.

Maria's glance meets his. The numbers unlock a somber resonance. As if keening, Gus closes his eyes and rocks on his heels. Maria places steadying hands on his shoulders, as both are swept into the eddying torrent of memory.

~~~~~~

September 11, 2001 8:40 a.m.

The dateline stamps the scenes of horror on CNN. A plane slices through the World Trade Tower. Conflagration! Immolation! Cataclysmic explosion! The roar of collapsing steel and shattering glass underscored by blaring sirens, human screams, the clatter of rescue teams rushing into the inferno.

White heat dissolves into a snowy stillness. A cloud of confetti and ash blankets the Financial District. Slow motion. Ghostly figures, barefoot, in business suits, dazedly search for an escape route.

White out. A graveyard of twisted girders and mounds of rubble. Behind the barriers, terror-stricken seekers hold signs with pictures of loved ones. " Have you seen my husband? My daughter? My brother?"

✳✳✳

Barely a mile away on the other side of the Hudson, the air is already acrid with the stench of charred human flesh. The neat rows of urban Colonials sit in silent shock. The whirr of Air Force jets overhead, patrolling the locked down city, jars the sepulchral silence.

As shadows lengthen, Gus sits crumpled, head in hands, on a garden bench in his elegantly landscaped rear yard. Twilight has activated the row of solar lights, illuminating the red and white rose bushes that climb the brick wall.

In the house, Maria goes about a few chores to numb her racing mind. She gathers up some linens and carries the laundry basket to the basement. As she is crossing the spacious recreation room where Gus keeps his treadmill and dressing room, she sees something that stops her cold! She gasps, drops the basket, and stares in disbelief at the ceiling. There, looped like a noose over a heavy pipe is Gus' belt!

Maria seizes the belt and rushes out the back door of the house, frantically calling for Gus. Seeing him on the bench, she stops short and sucks in a sob of relief. She walks slowly, softly toward him, gently places the belt on the bench next to him, *and kneels down. Gus does not stir. Maria gathers him into her arms.*

"My God, Gus! Why? What is it? Tell me!"

With a shudder, Gus' taut body goes limp. He collapses against his wife's breast, laying his head on her shoulder, sobbing," I don't know. Help me!"

Chapter Two

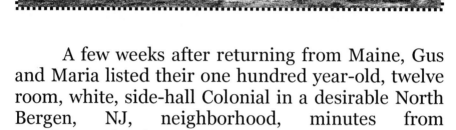

A few weeks after returning from Maine, Gus and Maria listed their one hundred year-old, twelve room, white, side-hall Colonial in a desirable North Bergen, NJ, neighborhood, minutes from Manhattan by ferry. Choosing a realtor had been dispiriting. According to Gus, realtors inhabited a circle of hell just above that of used car salesmen.

The real estate market had plunged shortly after the Sundergaards had bought their Meadowbrook land. The wonderful old house, which they had lovingly restored during the twelve years they lived in it, had been their first owned home – so vagabond had been their pre-forty years. The profit margin they had hoped for would now be greatly reduced, but neither Gus nor Maria had hesitated. Just before their September trip to Brunswick, Gus had confronted Maria with the rhetorical question.

"Should we go through with building right now?

To which, not missing a beat, Maria had replied, "We can't do anything else. It is too important for our future."

And so, for seven months, strangers wandered in and out of their domain. Weekends were spent cleaning and concealing pets. Maria channeled her nervousness into elaborate, even obsessive planning for the move. Gus let his stress smolder until it sometimes erupted in irritability and anger.

And still they moved forward. A phone call from Rob Ashland was a cause for celebration.

"Rob," Gus would assure the unfailingly polite young man, "you haven't interrupted our dinner. Your call has been the highlight of our day."

And they would design every detail of their new abode: the flooring, the appliances, the magnificent Wolf stove Gus had always coveted, the hand painted Sheepscot Pottery tile Maria had chosen, the doors, the lighting fixtures, the paint colors. And they watched from afar and on a few whirlwind Maine visits as their castle rose from the pine forest. It was a labor of love and affirmation of a shared lifetime of struggling, striving, and surviving.

Gus and Maria counted the months, the days, as they went about their usual routines. Old habits, old demons sometimes surfaced, but the forward propulsion was so strong that these were quickly banished.

✳✳✳

It is a chilly night in February 2008, shortly after Gus and Maria had accepted an offer for the sale of their North Bergen house. In his large elegant kitchen with its Wedgwood blue and white tile, wainscoting, and high-end appliances, Gus is at work preparing a gourmet dinner. His white shirt sleeves rolled up, still wearing his suit trousers, he sports a whimsical red chef's apron with a Polish inscription, a gift from his maternal Aunt Kapinos. A bottle of Kendall Jackson Reserve is open, and Gus sips some chardonnay from a Riedel glass.

He glances with annoyance at the clock – 7:30 p.m. – and takes another sip of wine, while stirring his concoction. As he adds a few drops of the chardonnay to the pan, the back door opens, and Maria trudges in. She is wearing her black cashmere coat, red suit, white silk blouse, and heels. She plops down her overstuffed briefcase on a chair and out falls a poster of her employer, opera singer Michael Hampton. Visibly frazzled and tired, she greets Gus dully.

"Hi, hon, I'm finally home."

Gus' *Hello* is chilly.

Trying not to notice, Maria gathers her things and heads through the French doors to the front closet. Seizing the opportunity for a forbidden sally, Caribou, a red tabby Maine Coon, scoots past Maria into the kitchen. Returning, Maria scoops the huge feline up and escorts him out of the kitchen, closing the French doors. She pours herself a glass of wine and refills Gus'. She sips the chardonnay appreciatively and slips noiselessly behind her husband, sniffing the aroma of his culinary creation.

"What are you making?"

"Wild mushroom risotto," Gus replies, as he tastes some and thrusts the spoon at Maria. She nibbles at it.

"Hmm, good, but you shouldn't have fussed. We could have had something simple. It's late."

Sullenly, Gus retorts, "You always say that and not because it's late. Because you don't appreciate the art of making a good meal. Sometimes, I think you don't appreciate anything I do."

"Not true. You know that, Gus."

Gus spoons the risotto onto two plates and sprinkles them with some freshly grated Parmeggiano Reggiano. He brings the dishes to the table and sits. Maria joins him, carrying the wine glasses. Gus sips his chardonnay and samples the risotto. The flavors gratify him, and he relaxes into a more amiable tone.

"So, let's change the subject. How was the recording session? Was the Countess there?" he asks, referring to Hampton's flamboyant companion, Austrian aristocrat by marriage and *arriviste* by nature, Arianne von Hartstein.

Maria laughs. "Oh, yeah, with all the ducklings in tow." Gus smiles at the reference to the three blond, picture-perfect Hartstein children. "*Die Gräfin* was trying to give the producer directions and whispering corrections to Michael at every break. I thought Mike was going to lose it. But he managed to tune her out, and we did get some great takes. We should be able to wrap it up before he heads back to Vienna on Friday. Then once he has gone, we'll have more time for ourselves. Let's do something nice this weekend. It's the first one without an open house! Do you want to go to Carnegie Hall? Flicka is giving a recital. I can get us comps."

Gus, who has been withdrawn all evening, momentarily perks up at the thought. "Frederica von Stade?" Then, remembering, "Oh, I wish I could, but I'm leaving for San Diego on Sunday."

His words hit Maria like a sledgehammer. She cannot disguise her panic at the separation. "I thought you said you were flying out on Monday?"

"I can't," Gus answers wearily. "I won't get there in time for the first session. And I have to get some sleep because I have a breakfast meeting with Charlie and a new money manager before the conference starts on Monday."

All her old fears, all the loneliness, and hateful arguments come flooding back to her, and she cannot prevent what escapes her lips: " You always do this! You tell me one thing and then change it! I can't wait until we are out of here! At least one of us will be retired and not always racing around the universe!"

She catches herself and interrupts the brewing tirade. Feigning a let's-change-the-subject-perkiness, she remarks," I wonder what Michael will do without me?" She expects Gus to switch gears with her, but he seems moored in his foul humor.

"Yeah, that's great!" he challenges her with rising bitterness. "You get to sit home and enjoy

Maine, and I get to kill myself for another three years."

Maria recognizes the danger signs. She begins to pacify. "It won't be that bad. You'll be working from home, no commuting, less stress, and we'll have lots more time for each other."

Her words are lost on her husband. Gus is busy working himself up into a fit of indignation. "You know what the moron, Bert James, told me today? They are not going to hire my replacement now because they need to cut costs, so I'll have no one to delegate to and I'll be handling two jobs with the bond portfolio and the regular investments."

Maria continues to placate. "Yeah, but they will need you even more then, and you can call all the shots."

"They don't listen most of the time," her husband counters morosely.

"Well, they listened last year when you told them you had another offer. We wouldn't be moving to Maine this spring if you hadn't engineered a sweet deal with them." Soothingly, she adds, "You handled them brilliantly, Gus."

Her praise, so deeply craved, softens Gus' mood. He is about to relent when several raucously meowing Maine Coons begin to scratch at the French doors. Like lightning, Gus loses his patience. "Damn it! Shut them up, will you?"

Recognizing the familiar sore subject, Maria soft pedals. "They're just hungry, and they miss us.

Let them in. I'll feed them, and you finish your wine."

Gus is clearly not amused and continues belligerently, "I can't wait until we move to Maine, and they'll have their own dining room." Maria clears the plates and does not answer. Her silence causes Gus to explode.

"Who the fuck has a house with this many cats? Most normal people have a dog. ONE dog!!" He gets up to pour himself another glass of wine and stands at the sink, staring out the window. Robotically, as if for the hundredth time, he asks, "Are we ever going to get out of this breeding game?"

Maria slips behind Gus, presses her body against his and enfolds him in her arms. She can feel his tension and begins to plead softly, "Oh, Gus, not that again, please. I know you don't enjoy it the way you did at first, but I thought we had agreed that it is still important to me. And besides, they are our family."

Gus is defeated. He reluctantly lets the argument go and relaxes into her embrace. But his eyes betray a helpless confusion, resolution still ridden with conflict.

Chapter Three

May 1, 2008. Moving day at last!

The months of planning, the little notebook filled with lists, the "what-if" scenarie, all Maria's work was finally coming to fruition. And almost without a hitch, that is, until two days ago.

The movers had arrived as scheduled to pack, but after only a few hours, they walked off the job, citing allergies to the cats, who had been confined to tents as promised. No legal threats from Gus or tears from Maria could get the crew back. In desperation, Gus furiously continued the packing, while Maria called the other van line that had given her a quote. After a few frantic phone exchanges, yes, Mayflower could finish the job, but the moving van would not be available for yet another day.

Gus was remarkably sanguine. He had not even made any snide remarks about the cats' causing the glitch. In fact, he was effusively warm to his wife. Gus marveled at Maria's "save." "It's incredible, honey, how you've arranged this whole move!"

Maria enjoyed the praise, but worst-case scenario were always part of her contingency plans. From the days she directed for the theatre, she had learned to have backup props, understudies, and a mental rehearsal for every unforeseen disaster – falling scenery, unscripted blackouts, missed cues, whatever! Her foresight had been useful in the decades with Hampton: backup travel plans for tours, extra copies of scores, checked and double-checked itineraries. Hampton had never seemed to appreciate this; he almost always seemed annoyed that things went like clockwork. Improvisation was his forte, not Maria's.

On their extra day in North Bergen, Gus and Maria took a long walk down the main street, Bergenline Avenue, and through the heart of West New York, the gritty, blue-collar city where Maria had grown up. They paid a last visit to her grandparents' house on 59th Street, the two-story quotidian brick edifice Carlo had built not long after emigrating from Italy; the house in which her mother, Donna, Aunt Re and Uncle Frank had passed their childhoods; the walled garden with the fig trees where Maria and her cousins had romped as youngsters, playing pretend games like "Brave Ladies"; the house where Gus and Maria as newlyweds had enjoyed Peppina's *cucina* and collected her recipes for a book they would later write on Calabrian food.

They ended their walk in North Hudson Park, circling the duck pond and resting on a bench in the late afternoon sun. They had agreed that this oasis of green, a few blocks from their home, might be the only thing they would miss. The city with its crowds, traffic, relentless noise, and glittering amusements had lost its charm.

✳✳✳

Gus steps back from the van and tests the straps on the roof rack, as Maria does a quick head count and closes the hatch back.

"Whew!" she chuckles, surveying the ten cat carriers with their wide-eyed inhabitants all fastened down for the seven-hour trip. "That took some strategic preparation. "Let's hope they behave, or this is going to be the trip from hell!"

"Look out, Meadowbrook," Gus wisecracks as he studies the van loaded to the maximum. "Here come the Joads!" Maria laughs at his Steinbeck reference. He stands back and slips his arm around his wife's waist. They take a last look at their old home.

Gus is the first to speak. "Twelve years in this house."

"So many lifetimes," Maria murmurs, "and the best is about to begin." She pretends not to notice the tiny tear in Gus' eye as they climb into their car and pull away without looking back. The van's rear bumper signals its own adieu. The sticker reads, *Maine, the way life should be.*

Chapter Four

It is just 4:00 p.m. when Gus, Maria, their menagerie, and the Mannahatta mobile pull into the driveway of 12 Tamarack Drive. The trip has been uneventful. Despite months of dreading the ride, there has not been a peep from the cats, no carsickness or worse! The miles have raced by – the crowded metropolitan highways giving way to the spacious, tree-lined Maine Turnpike, and finally to the welcoming sights of Brunswick.

Keys in hand, Rob Ashland is waiting for them on the front porch of their Nantucket grey and white ranch. "Welcome! Was your trip OK?" he asks.

"We're finally here," Maria offers. "We all made it in one piece."

"Yes," Gus jokes, "surprisingly uneventful with that carload."

Looking at the van with its lettered sign, *Mannahatta Maine Coons*, Rob is too polite to comment. He hands Gus the keys.

Maria gushes, "Thanks, Rob, for everything. It is just beautiful," she adds, taking a long look.

"I wish you much happiness. Call me for anything you need," Rob says with genuine neighborliness. Somewhat shyly, he pulls from his pocket a small digital camera. "Do you mind? I

always like to take a picture. It brings good luck."
He motions to Gus and Maria to pose on the front
portico.   Arms around each other's waists, the
Sundergaards beam smiles as the camera flashes.

For an instant time stands still before racing
back through the decades.

~~~~~~

*Another much larger flash bulb goes off.
Another decade. FLASH, FLASH. A momentous
memory. FLASH. October 18, 1969. A wedding.
Gösta Sundergaard is twenty-three years-old and
his bride, Maria Vivaldi is twenty-two. They stand
holding hands in the center of a semicircle of
plainly crafted wooden benches in the candlelit
Ridgewood Friends Meeting House, as the wedding
photographer takes a few more poses before the
ceremony begins.*

*The guests have begun to arrive, a modest
gathering of family and old friends. The bride's
and groom's parents occupy the center front bench.
The Vivaldis and Sundergaards are conspicuously
overdressed in the assemblage of somber business
attire and 60s hippie chic. The fathers both wear
tuxedos with ruffled shirts and large bow ties, the
mothers in long satin gowns in too bright colors. It
is apparent that they feel uncomfortable, not only
because of their apparel, but because of the place.
All four would rather be at Latin High Mass in a
cathedral.*

In contrast to their parents, Gus and Maria look radiant. Maria's tall, slim figure is shown to advantage in the simple, ankle length, sky blue velvet dress, which her father, a designer, has sewn for her. Her dark black hair piled in curls on her head, her makeup accentuating her Mediterranean features, she reminds people of a young Maria Callas, one of her idols. Gus – with longish blonde hair, sideburns and bushy moustache – sports an inexpensive double-breasted grey suit, a new addition to his otherwise casual closet. Each is wearing his betrothed's wedding gift: Maria a gold heart necklace and Gus gold cufflinks emblazoned with the peace sign.

The four Quaker witnesses take their places on the side left bench. The meetinghouse falls silent, as everyone, including bride and groom, meditate in silent expectation of an inner stirring, a sense of the Light Within that reveals truth and urges action.

After a brief interval, almost simultaneously, Maria and Gus rise, signaling that they are prepared to take their vows. Maria opens a well-worn copy of Elizabeth Barrett Browning's <u>Sonnets to the Portuguese</u> and begins to read from "Sonnet XLIII."

"How do I love thee? Let me count the ways..." Halfway through the poem, she looks up directly into Gus' eyes, closes the book, and continues from memory, her voice confident from years of theatre training, though she falters a little *on the last line: "And if God choose, I shall but love thee better after death."*

When she finishes, she smiles encouragingly at Gus, who opens his Browning copy, Maria's first birthday gift to him, and replies with "Sonnet VI." He is overcome by the time he murmurs the closing lines: "What I do/And what I dream include thee, As the wine must taste of its own grapes/And when I sue God for myself/He hears that name of thine, /And sees within my eyes the tears of two."

He reaches into his pocket and slips a slim, burnished gold band on Maria's left hand and, haltingly, then more confidently, he recites the traditional Quaker marriage vow: "I, Gösta Sundergaard, take thee, Maria Vivaldi, to be my loving wife, promising with Divine Assistance to be unto thee a loving and faithful husband as long as we both shall live."

Maria puts a wider version of the same band on Gus' finger and repeats the same vow. In the pinkish gold aura of the candlelight, they remain still, hands joined, eyes radiant, before Gus bends forward to kiss his bride. FLASH! The photographer freezes this image of young love: passion, happiness, limitless hope.

CLICK! FLASH! CLICK! With each advancing frame a rush of recall.

April 1969. Just six months earlier. In a shabby storefront on Cedar Lane in Teaneck, NJ, twenty-one-year-old Sarah Lawrence student, Maria Vivaldi, mans a mimeograph machine, industriously churning out leaflets. There is ink all over her hands, and she works as if she alone has the duty to notify all of New Jersey about the October 15, 1969, Moratorium and March on Washington. She is so absorbed in her task that she doesn't notice the blond young man in plaid shirt and tattered bell-bottoms pause to read the sign outside.

Gus Sundergaard has stopped in front of The Peace Center to read the window poster: "Draft Counselor Wanted." His convictions compel him to offer his services, but, then, so too, perhaps, does his first sight of Maria. Tall, slim, her black mini skirt and plain white knit top, her long black hair piled up casually on her head, her horn-rimmed glasses and serious but sexy air pull him in.

"Hello, I saw your sign," Gus murmurs.

Not missing a beat on the mimeograph, Maria looks up. There is no special greeting in her eyes.

Gus adds, "I see you are looking for a draft counselor. I've been working at Penn State — "

She gestures toward the inner office, visible through a glass partition. "You'll have to see Barry. This is his place. He's in there."

Gus nods politely, knocks on the glass, and is beckoned in. Maria resumes mimeographing, but inexplicably, her eyes follow Gus. She watches as he introduces himself to the two men who have been leaning over an old wooden desk studying a map of the Mall in Washington, D.C. Then she glances to the curb, where a red Triumph T4 is parked. Bemused, she looks back at its owner and smiles to herself at the incongruity.

"I was told I needed to see Barry Morris," Gus inquires. "I can help you with the draft counseling."

"I'm Barry," the short, middle-aged man replies. He smiles and shakes Gus' hand. "This is Jesse Mills."

Barry wears an intense expression. He is a prominent businessman in the town, lives in the best section, and has a society conscious wife and pretty teenaged daughter. He has made a fortune in printing, but now at mid-life, he feels alienated from his family's milieu. He uses much of his business profit to fund liberal causes and has built The Peace Center into a state-wide grass roots organization which initiates anti-war activism and supports doves as political candidates.

Jesse Mills, his chief organizer, is a twenty-five year-old, African American graduate student who has grown up in the Civil Rights Movement. He has a brash, youthful energy and an uncompromising drive and commitment.

"You're just in time," Barry adds. "We can surely use some help."

Gus looks pleased. "I did quite a bit of counseling at Penn State before I dropped out."

Barry raises his eyebrows as if to ask why. Gus offers an explanation without being asked: "Crazy, huh? Well, engineering wasn't for me. It was what my old man wanted. If it had been up to me, I'd have majored in philosophy. Anyway, it seemed a waste of time to be holed up on campus when there is so much important work to be done out here. To stop the war, I mean."

Jesse smiles. Gus sounds like a man after his own heart – action, courage. "Right, man!" He indicates the map on the desk. "We need every committed person we can get. Look at these plans for October."

Barry puts his arm paternally around Gus' shoulder, and the three lean over the map, tracing the march route.

Maria, who has not taken her eyes off Gus while still mechanically mimeographing, is brought down off her cloud by the machine's running out of paper. As she tussles to feed the monster, Gus leaves Barry's office. She looks up and engages his eyes. She is not prepared for the steely blue intensity which meets hers. She thrusts a leaflet at Gus. "See you there?" she asks weakly.

"For sure," Gus stammers. He turns to go but then turns back. "Gus. Gus Sundergaard." He stands there awkwardly before breaking into a boyish smile.

"Maria. Maria Vivaldi." She, too, smiles brightly. "See you."

Chapter Five

And see each other they did, not just on October 15th, but everyday from their April meeting until their October 18th wedding!

At first, they shared their activism; they handed out leaflets at the Draft Board, set up counseling tables in the Mall, wrote and delivered anti-war speeches to Congressional candidates. They talked passionately about politics. Maria had worked in Bobby Kennedy's campaign, and Gus had been part of the SDS. He had almost burned his draft card, but meeting Maria had caused him to consider a more judicious protest. He filed as a Conscientious Objector, but his claim was rejected. He was I-A, and he was desperately in love. Time was running out, and Gus knew he did not have the luxury of a long courtship.

Normally shy with women, he took the plunge. He asked Maria for a real date, to go with him to the movies. The film was Zefferelli's <u>Romeo and Juliet</u>, and after being enraptured by the on screen lovers, Gus had put his arm around Maria's shoulders and walked her to the Triumph. He opened the door for her; they got in, and then he leaned over and kissed her. To his amazement, Maria kissed him back!

The summer of 1969 sped by: marches, protests, dates. Gus had a genius for creating a romantic evening. He spent every penny he had saved while working odd jobs during college. Once when his parents were away, he fêted Maria with a candlelit dinner of champagne and lobster thermador he had prepared himself. Another weekend they went to The Village Gate to see <u>Jacques Brel Is Alive and Well and Living in Paris</u> and then ate at the tiny Italian bistro, Portofino. They heard Bob Dylan and Joan Baez at the Bitter End Cafe. They ate zeppole and gelati at the Feast of San Gennaro in Little Italy, and then on that September evening during the ride home, Gus proposed.

He couldn't afford a ring. Did she mind? He might have to go to jail, would she wait? Or Canada, together? To these and, indeed, to the most important of all his questions, "Did she love him as he did her," Maria answered, "Yes."

Gus was delirious at his good fortune; both were afraid there was no time to lose. He had already passed the physical. He had two appeals, but then what? Maria had a few more months before her January graduation. They decided to marry the next month after the Moratorium and March and face the future together.

Chapter Six

October 15, 1969. The Mall, Washington, D.C. is packed with people, young, old, black, white, veterans and draft resisters, celebrities and politicians. The organizers' work has paid rich dividends. One hundred thousand people and everything proceeding according to plan in a peaceful, orderly way.

✳✳✳

On a side street near the Capitol, Barry, Jesse, Gus, and Maria lead a New Jersey contingent. Arms cross-locked, they march toward the Mall singing "We Shall Overcome." They pause at an intersection as a marshal directs traffic. The stop prompts Gus to steal a kiss.

"Only three more days," he whispers to Maria.

She smiles mischievously. "And here we are, instead of picking flower arrangements and fitting tuxes and a wedding dress." They had chosen, over the violent objections of their parents, Friends Meeting for their wedding, and they had deliberately insisted that the festivities be kept small and simple. "Our mothers are probably

*having nervous breakdowns at this very moment."
The idea seems amusing to both of them.*

*Maria smiles again remembering the
September night when she had come home late
from their date and announced to Donna Vivaldi
that she and Gus intended to wed. Donna became
hysterical. She ranted about Maria's leaving her,
screamed about Gus' lack of prospects, accused
Maria of ingratitude, of throwing away all
advantages of the prestigious education she and
John had scrimped and saved to give their
daughter. Donna woke John and begged him to
get up and DO something! John had pulled the
pillow over his head and tuned his wife out, a
method he had perfected in over thirty years of
marriage. Donna had finally called her sister,
Marietta, who managed to talk some sense into the
situation. "For heavens sake, Donna," she scolded,
"Maria's getting married. It's not a tragedy!"*

*Gus' announcement at his home had met with
a similar, if more controlled reaction. His father,
Nils, already furious with Gus for dropping out of
college and for his activism, knew his son would
not be deterred. He received the news in stony
silence and then curtly requested that the couple
choose a date that would not conflict with his golf
engagements. Nils' wife, Vilma, on the other hand,
had "an attack of the vapors," and took to her bed
for a week, refusing to speak to Gus. She was most
distraught that Gus' bride was Italian and not
Polish like her family and that neither her son nor*

his intended would consent to a Catholic wedding. She tormented herself and Nils with her belief that in leaving the Church, Gus and Maria would be damned and so would any of their children who would not be baptized.

In the end, both sets of parents had put on stoic faces for the sake of appearances and proceeded with the inevitable.

✳✳✳

Maria shakes her reverie as the marshal blows his whistle and signals their group to cross. Singing, they make their way to join the fervent crowds. On the podium Peter, Paul, and Mary are performing "Where have all the flowers gone?" When they finish, they direct the crowd's attention to large screens for a visual presentation.

The slides flash through recent events: hellacious footage of jungle warfare in Vietnam; draft protesters staging a sit-in; young men burning draft cards; Martin Luther King delivering his "I have a dream" speech; Dr. King crumpled on the balcony in Memphis; Bobby Kennedy at the Ambassador Hotel moments before his assassination.

The images sear themselves into Gus and Maria's souls.

Chapter Seven

On an afternoon in late May 2008, Gus and Maria revisit these images.

"Remember this one? " Maria asks as she hammers a hook into the wall of their new study in Brunswick. She hangs the worn news photo of the Mall during the 1969 Moratorium.

"I remember spending the night in the back of my father's camper," teases Gus.

"They are like old friends," Maria says. "They've been with us in every place we have ever lived for thirty-nine years. She stands back with Gus to survey the wall arrangement. He slips his arm loosely around her waist.

"Any particular order?" he queries. Maria gestures left to right.

"Oldest to most recent. This one is before we met." She points to the 1968-autographed photo of Robert Francis Kennedy campaigning. It is inscribed: *To Maria, Thanks for your tireless work, Bobby.* She sighs. She can still feel the sorrow of that June 5th night; it was the instant she had lost faith in the political process and been catapulted into the Movement.

"Our first demonstration together." Gus points to a photo of the Reverend Jesse Jackson and other Civil Rights activists leading marchers down Pennsylvania Ave.

"Your first arrest," Maria twits. She has hung the framed newspaper clipping from November 5, 1969. The headline from *The Bergen Record* reads *Anti-War Demonstrators Stage Draft Board Sit-In. Organizer Arrested.* Beneath the headline is a large photo of twenty-three year-old Gus being led away by the Hackensack police, his left hand in the air pumping a peace sign.

"Your mother loved that one, remember?" Gus needles Maria. "She collected all the newspapers off the neighbors' porches and threw them away before they could read what a low-life her new son-in-law was!"

"It was just a few days after we had come back from our honeymoon," Maria laughs. "We had nothing, but we were so, so happy."

She glances at the middle group of photos: she and Gus in their thirties in front of San Marco, Venice, and then a decade later posed in evening dress outside the Wagner Festspielhaus in Bayreuth. As her eyes fall on a photo from ten years earlier of Gus and her posed with several of their show cats, she adds, "But then, we always made our own happiness, even in the difficult years."

She pauses a second and changes the subject. "And here we are just last year, me with Hampton at the Met and you on Wall Street for the closing bell. And now we are here, Maine."

Gus shakes his head, almost in disbelief. "Sometimes, I feel as if I am standing beside myself, watching a movie. I can't believe we actually made it. Do you feel like that?"

"Oh, no, love," Maria replies. "I have imagined us like this for so long that it feels familiar. We are home, Gus – home forever." She throws her arms around his neck and kisses him.

Chapter 8

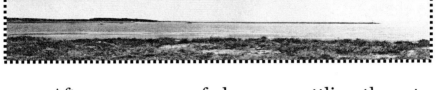

After a summer of chores – settling the cats, unpacking the boxes, hanging the curtains, decorating the house, clearing brush, landscaping, and gardening, Gus and Maria are finally able to relax.

For September 11, 2008, Gus' sixty-second birthday, Maria suggests they celebrate at home, just the two of them. She sets the table with their white linens, Spode china, and Waterford crystal, and lights the candles. She opens a bottle of Schramsberg and pours the flutes.

Gus brings his culinary creation to the table. "Surprise," he grins. "Real lobster thermador for me and a vegetarian version for you."

Maria raises her glass and clinks his. "Happy birthday, love."

Gus has tears in his eyes and reaches for her hand. "Yes, finally happy again."

"It's the first time in a long while that we've celebrated on your real birthday, Gus. No more curse of 9/11. We've left that all behind. The stars have gotten it right this time."

They are quiet for a few minutes savoring their food. Then she continues, "Funny, isn't it? We bought the land on your birthday. We closed on our anniversary; we began to build on my birthday, and here we are, all settled in on yours, with the best yet to come."

They fall silent again, enjoying the warm candle glow, the crisp bubbly wine, the delicious meal, and their sense of utter contentment. When they finish eating, Maria breaks the stillness.

"Do you want your present now?

"Being here together is the best present," her husband answers.

"Just the two of us?" Maria teases.

Gus misses her meaning. "Yes, why?"

Maria hands him a birthday card. "Wouldn't three be nicer?"

A picture of an adorable eight-week-old Newfoundland puppy falls out of the envelope. Gus is stunned. His brow furrows. Maria is unsure of his reaction.

"Rufus?" Gus murmurs.

"Rufus?" Maria echoes.

"He's had a name for a long time," Gus admits sheepishly. Maria is relieved, and they exchange smiles. "Actually," Gus continues, "Midship's Sea Dog Rufus. He's going to be a champion, so he needs a serious name."

"He's going to be our baby," Maria corrects.

"Aren't we too old to be raising a child?" Gus wonders.

"Older, but wiser," his wife reassures him. "Mostly wiser."

Gus becomes instantly sad. "Wish we had been wiser then."

"Me, too," Maria whispers, patting his hand. "But I was afraid then that I would screw it up. That I'd have been my mother." She hesitates but then adds candidly, "And you were afraid, too."

Gus finishes her thought: "Of losing the special thing we had, just the two of us – no one else. I guess we just let time get away from us. When we were finally ready, it was too late."

"That's why the cats have meant so much to me these past fifteen years. They've filled a void."

"I know," Gus concedes.

Maria brightens. "But now is a good time. We can have our little boy."

"Not so little, really." Gus' blue eyes twinkle.

Maria is caught off guard. "Would our child have had those blue eyes?" she asks herself.

Chapter Nine

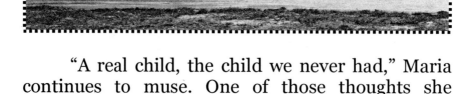

"A real child, the child we never had," Maria continues to muse. One of those thoughts she should let go. But she cannot.

A Sunday in 1972. Dinner with Gus' parents in their neat little suburban Cresskill, NJ, bungalow, a house Gus' father, Nils, remodeled and expanded beam by beam for his growing family. Gus remembers how he and his brother, Anselm, were pressed into service as carpenter's helpers, while his sisters, Ingrid and Helmi, got to go play outside. Nils would teach his boys manly skills like sawing and hammering.

Born in Minnesota of Norwegian immigrant parents, Nils Sundergaard became an Air Force pilot in WWII, flying B-52 missions over Italy. Returning home in 1945, he married Vilma, his Polish Catholic sweetheart, returned to Minnesota, studied engineering on the GI bill, started a family, and upon taking his degree, moved East to accept a job in New York City.

The foursome is finishing plotzak and coffee in an awkward silence. Nils sits erect and stern. In his house he is used to giving orders and having

*them obeyed, voicing his opinion as law. Vilma –
pretty, plump, artificially blond – never
contradicts her husband. This is domestic
contentment according to Nils Sundergaard. This
is not the life his wayward son, Gus, has chosen,
and Nils does not hide his disapproval.*

*The relationship between the elder and
younger Sundergaards has been rocky since Gus
and Maria's wedding. Nils has vehemently
disapproved of Gus' dropout, conscientious
objector status. He has called his son a coward and
a draft-dodger, comparing Gus unfavorably to
Anselm, who is serving in the Air Force. When Gus
and Maria went to live in Toronto for several
months in 1970 after Maria's graduation from
Sarah Lawrence, Nils had disowned them. When
the Canadian experiment failed – Maria and Gus
running out of money before they could get jobs –
he refused even temporary shelter to the returning
prodigals. It fell to John Vivaldi to lend Gus and
Maria a modest $100 toward a rental apartment
and to Anselm, who, without his father's approval
or knowledge, helped his brother and sister-in-law
resettle themselves.*

*Gus had foresworn seeing his parents for
almost two years, until Vilma had begged him to
reconcile with his father. By 1972 Maria was
successfully teaching English and theatre and Gus
had returned to night school, while earning a living
by day in a local chemical plant office. The
Selective Service Lottery had spared Gus long*

enough to use his draft counseling skills to find himself a loophole: he located a dove orthodontist to fit him with braces, a temporary deferment. History did the rest, so that by 1974 Gus and Maria would finally be free of their Vietnam nightmare.

But on this particular Sunday evening, so soon after reconciling with his parents, Gus finds himself again alienated. Dinner had begun with recriminations, and by dessert a full-blown dispute had erupted. Maria now sits with her eyes lowered, fighting back tears. Gus reaches for her hand under the table, a surreptitious solidarity.

Vilma, unable to contain herself, scolds Maria. "All I know is that it is not normal! Married women of your age want to start a family!"

Nils interrupts because, of course, he can handle this better than his wife. He begins in a quiet, sanctimonious tone, but quickly loses his patience. "What Mother is trying to say, Gus, is that it is your duty in this life to bring children into the world and raise them. It is the natural order. You would know that if you hadn't turned your back on your Church and associated yourself with those Quakers! Son," he sputters, "when are you going to grow up and get a real paying job and stop protesting things you cannot change!"

Maria comes to Gus' defense. "But, Dad, that's not fair."

Gus cuts her off. He knows that Maria's asserting herself will only make Nils angrier. "Sh-sh, Maria, not now."

Hearing her beloved son berated, however, Vilma cannot keep silent. "Nils, don't blame Gus. There is something wrong with a woman who wants a career and doesn't want to stay home and take care of her husband and family. If she had a family!"

"There is something wrong with a man who can't control his wife!" Nils explodes.

Gus can take no more. He stands up, pushes his plate away and mutters through gritted teeth: "I think it's getting late. We'll be going. Good night, Mother, Father."

Vilma dissolves into tears. "I want grandchildren. I just want grandchildren," she moans piteously.

Without another word, Gus hastens Maria to the front door. Niles shouts after Gus: "Grow up, son. Be a man!"

In reply, the door slams loudly.

Chapter Ten

A few nights after Gus' sixty-second birthday, he and Maria are sitting up in bed, sipping brandy, and leafing through the piles of dog catalogs. Rufus is obviously becoming a reality.

Maria shows Gus a page from *In the Company of Dogs*. "What do you think of this kennel? We're not allowed chain link fences here in Meadowbrook. But this is black oxidized aluminum.

Hmmn, Diamond Pro. Well, it's pricey, but why not," Gus agrees. "Nothing but the best for our boy."

Indicating another catalog, Maria pursues the theme. "Which of these raised feeders do you like? They say it's important to prevent bloat."

"The adjustable one, I think. This way it grows with him."

Maria marks the page and continues the virtual shopping. "And we have to get him this life jacket." She points at a yellow flotation device. "It's the biggest one."

"What does he need a life jacket for? Newfs are natural water dogs," Gus protests.

"But I read that it helps him to learn to swim correctly." Maria hints, "I was thinking we could take him for swim lessons at Doggie Dome Spa during the winter."

Half teasing, half exasperated, her husband retorts, "Why don't we see if we can enroll him in prep school, too?"

Maria reaches over and tweaks Gus' nose. "Stop!" The pair continues to peruse the vast array of equipment available for pampered puppies: crates, ramps, toys, collars. They dogear pages and exchange catalogs.

"Oh, he's got to have this toy," Maria coos.

"His very own moose!" Gus laughs as he sees the oversized plush squeaky toy Maria has picked.

"Well, we are in Maine," Maria rejoins.

Chapter Eleven

In the next few weeks, 12 Tamarack Drive is abuzz with puppy preparations. UPS arrives with boxes of supplies every day. Closets are reorganized, cat food and litter repositioned safely, the bedroom puppy-proofed. Maria hauls out her old sewing machine to make crate covers and mats, bibs and bandanas.

Gus takes advantage of the glorious fall weather to clear a site near their woods for Rufus' kennel. He insists on building the wooden base himself. On the Sunday before they are to pick up the puppy, Gus is hammering the last planks into place. Maria jumps on the base to test its durability.

"My God, Gus, a helicopter could land here!" she jokes.

"Here, give me a hand putting up these panels," Gus asks. They work side by side for the next hour, Maria holding the kennel walls upright for Gus to bolt them together. She actually enjoys this kind of hands on work. It brings her back her days of building stage sets or all the renovations she and Gus did to their North Bergen home.

"Remember, Gus," she asks, "when we built Friskie's rooms?" She is referring to the safe haven attached to their garage which they erected to house the four abandoned felines Gus had rescued from their backyard.

"Friskie's Feline Finishing School," he recalls. "It had a nice ring to it."

"And remember when it was all done, you got on the ladder to hang the carved sign over the door. And you drove the nail in, and all the electricity went out," Maria laughs.

Gus winces. "You have to remind me! What was the chance the nail would hit the wiring in the wall? It took us the rest of the day to open the wall, repair it, and close it up again!" he remembers as he snaps the last kennel wall into place.

"Can you get the roof up yourself while I go inside and get us some ice tea?" Maria asks.

"Yeah, go ahead."

By the time she returns with two tall glasses garnished with mint sprigs, Gus has fitted the shade roof onto its frame above the kennel. He takes the proffered glass, and they step back to look at Rufus' house, framed idyllically by the tall pines, its door opening onto a path through the flowerbeds.

"Speaking of hanging signs," Maria says, "put this one up, please." She hands Gus a little engraved plaque with the silhouette of a Newfoundland dog which reads *Hôtel du Newf - Chez Rufus*.

"So, where did you get this?" Gus asks.

"I designed and ordered it online."

A bemused twinkle in their eyes, they clink glasses. Gus toasts, "To us and to Rufus."

His wife returns the salute. "To raising Rufus!"

Chapter Twelve

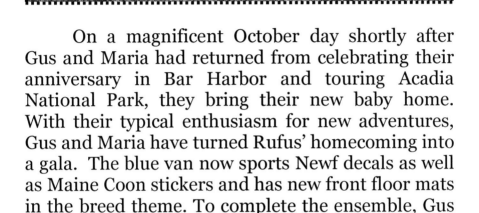

On a magnificent October day shortly after Gus and Maria had returned from celebrating their anniversary in Bar Harbor and touring Acadia National Park, they bring their new baby home. With their typical enthusiasm for new adventures, Gus and Maria have turned Rufus' homecoming into a gala. The blue van now sports Newf decals as well as Maine Coon stickers and has new front floor mats in the breed theme. To complete the ensemble, Gus and Maria are wearing sweatshirts with Newf silhouettes.

Getting out of the van, Maria sets the twenty-five-pound puppy on the front lawn. She addresses the fluffy bundle as if speaking to a child, "Here we are, Rufie. This is your new home. Look at all the space you'll have to play."

She hands the leash to Gus and goes to open the front door. As she fumbles for her keys, the puppy loses no time in taking a huge dump on the lawn.

Gus groans, "Here we go!"

"Oh, Gus, just take him in. I'll take care of it." Rufus bounds after Gus into his new domain.

✳✳✳

Throughout the fall and early winter of 2008, raising Rufus, indeed, occupies the lion's share of the Sundergaards' time. Maria continues her care of the cats and the first new litter of Maines born since the move, while Gus manages his portfolios during business hours. But before and after is Rufus time. Each day holds a new experience for the trio. And each week, Ruf the Newf, as Gus dubs him, morphs into a bigger and bigger beast – a goofy, lumbering, sometimes headstrong, mostly loveable black bear.

While yet relatively small, Rufus meets the Maine Coons. The initial introduction turns into a free for all – cats flying in all directions, cat bowls overturned, their contents inhaled by Rufus. At the next meeting Gus has Rufus on a leash while Maria uses a feather wand to distract the cats. Gus invites Rufus to approach politely the cat tree, but as the pup sniffs curiously, he receives a smart smack on the nose from Moosebec, a twenty-one pound, no nonsense bruiser. Rufus whines and retreats to the kitchen where he sulks, head on paws, feelings obviously wounded.

"After all, he's a puppy; he just wants to play," Maria excuses him.

And play Rufus does – fetch on the back lawn with Gus most afternoons at 4:00 p.m. As a beginning training exercise, Gus teaches the dog to return the ball or bumper directly to his hand, but sometimes the urge to cut loose is too great for Rufus, and he turns the repetitive game into a romp. Man and dog chase each other and finally roll together on the grass. The game ends when Rufus puts his paws on Gus' chest and enthusiastically licks his face.

On another unseasonably balmy autumn day, Maria fills a kiddie pool on the lawn and decides to introduce Rufie to water. Showing his stubborn streak, Rufus refuses to step in. Maria rolls up her trousers and stands into the pool. Taking a treat from her pocket, she beckons Rufus. The smell of the bacon bit overcomes the dog's resistance. He takes a running leap and plunges into the wading pool, knocking Maria over and thoroughly soaking everyone.

"His first swim," Gus announces gleefully.

By late fall, Rufus, now over one hundred pounds, accompanies Gus and Maria on their daily walk in the woods. The weather finally has the delicious crispness of the season, and the foliage on the hardwoods in the Brunswick Town Commons is gloriously variegated in shades of yellow, crimson, and burnt orange. Rufus forages for sticks and leaves. Maria worries he will swallow one and choke; Gus keeps reminding her, "He's a dog. They do that."

"And dogs, like horses," Maria retorts, "are disasters waiting to happen."

"How's that?" Gus seems weary of this discussion. "It just comes out the other end! Puppies eat anything they can get."

And, indeed, Rufus does try his luck at a favorite Newf pastime, counter surfing. By December he stands at his full height and weighs one hundred and twenty pounds, a strapping young male testing limits. Once a week, Gus, who needs no excuse to cook – even for a dog – insists that they bake homemade peanut butter cookies for Ruf. It becomes an early evening ritual when darkness in Maine descends at 4:30 p.m.

Gus, who has not used the elaborate Kitchen Aid mixer Maria had bought him almost a decade ago, suddenly finds it a wonderful tool to churn out dozens of cookies. With Maria's help, he mixes a triple batch of peanut butter, cornmeal, oatmeal, oil, and water, and rolls out the dough. Maria uses the Newf shaped cookie cutter to make the treats. Twenty minutes in the oven and *voilà*!

While the cookies are baking, they prep dinner. Gus pours a marinade over his pork cutlets and sets them on the counter; Maria assembles a salad with goat cheese. They pour themselves a little white wine and wait for the oven to be free.

In twenty minutes, Maria removes the two trays of Newf cookies and sets them on the counter to cool. She goes to set the dining room table for their dinner when suddenly Gus shouts, "No!" But he is too late. Rufus has swept the counter; he has inhaled a pork cutlet and is now stealing a still warm cookie. Maria whisks the cookie trays to higher ground.

"SIT, Rufus," she commands, giving the accompanying hand signal. Rufus does not comply.

"DOWN, Rufus," Gus essays.

No response. Rufus is licking his chops, clearly delighted with his appetizer of raw pork and peanut butter cookies. Gus and Maria look at each other simultaneously.

"Back to school?" Maria asks.

"Definitely back to school!" Gus affirms.

Chapter Thirteen

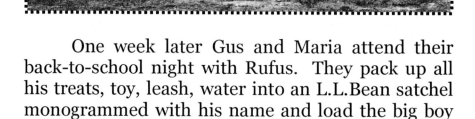

One week later Gus and Maria attend their back-to-school night with Rufus. They pack up all his treats, toy, leash, water into an L.L.Bean satchel monogrammed with his name and load the big boy into the van for the ride to Bath.

There are four other couples – mostly middle-aged – with their older puppies. Rufus is, of course, the largest, but he seems fascinated by the smaller dogs – the Shiba Inu, Aussie, Dachshund, and Jack Russell.

Patty, the teacher, calls everyone into a circle. This is a refresher course for pups on a second try at these basics. Rufus is eager to please, but he cannot help being a goofy, galumphing student.

"Have you all been practicing since you were last here?" Patty asks in a cheery tone. "Let's see what they remember." Gus grimaces. "Let's try "SIT, DOWN, STAY."

She walks around the circle to each dog and handler and scrutinizes the pups as they execute the sequence. When she stops in front of Rufus, the dog obliges perfectly. Gus seems relieved and rewards him with a treat. Patty is impressed. "Good! OK, then, let's line up and do some loose leash walking."

Maria takes her turn at handling Rufus. She walks him down and back across the mats on the gymnasium floor. It is hardly a smooth performance. Rufus pulls on the lead as if he were at a draft test, and Maria can barely keep up. As they come back to their place, Gus grabs the leash out of his wife's hand. "Let me do it! That's not how to heel," Gus barks in frustration. He repeats the pattern, and Rufus seems to respond more positively. "That's better," Gus says with self-satisfaction.

"OK," Patty signals. "Time for a little socialization. Turn them loose. They'll teach each other how to interact."

A free for all ensues. Rufus is all good nature, but he cannot help being overbearing. He charges around the gym, knocking over all the smaller dogs. He crashes through the ring fence and bounds about gleefully, being the big, bad boy.

Gus seems amused and snaps a photo. Maria looks worried and keeps wanting to intervene in the melee, though Gus restrains her. Finally, Patty calls an end to the chaos.

"That's it for tonight. Collect your dogs. See you next week. And practice!"

Gus and Maria almost have to tackle Rufus to leash him. The dog appears dismayed to leave and keeps tugging at the lead and whining for his chums. Gus hustles him into the backseat of the van and fastens the safety harness before he and Maria get in front. Gus puts the car in gear and pulls away with an assertiveness that reflects his conflicting feelings about the class.

"I was a little worried that he would hurt himself or someone else," Maria says.

"Oh, for God's sake, Maria, he's a puppy! He's supposed to run around. Stop treating him as if he were made of glass! You sound just like your mother!"

The remark wounds Maria. She bites her lip and looks out the window; she closes her eyes, her dark lashes turning a page from her memory.

~~~~~~

She is in Long Branch, NJ. It is the summer of 1954 when she is seven years old. Under the watchful eyes of her mother, the curly haired, doe-eyed little imp is splashing in the surf. Around her waist she is wearing a bright green inflated tube in the shape of a seahorse. Donna Vivaldi has placed her and her husband John's towels and umbrella at the water's edge, the better to keep an intense eye on her daughter. John Vivaldi is immersed in a book while Donna keeps checking her watch. Finally, she frowns and addresses her husband.

"John, she's been in the water almost twenty minutes now. She's going to catch a cold."

John does not look up from his reading. He simply utters one of his routine monosyllables, "Huh?"

"You're not listening to me, John," Donna intones sourly.

"Hmn. What?" His bland nonchalance prompts Donna to take charge of the situation.

"It's getting late anyway. We should be going home. I want Maria to go to bed early because she has a piano lesson first thing tomorrow morning, and she still has to practice tonight. By the time we drive home and she practices and we eat – "

Defeated, John cuts her off. "OK, OK. We'll go." He stands up and calls his daughter in. "Come on, honey. Your mom says we have to go."

Maria turns reluctantly to her dad. Her quivering lip and eyes filled with little-girl disappointment are a silent plea. Mechanically, John beckons again. "Let's go."

She obeys.

~~~~~~

As Maria turns from the window toward Gus, she is wearing that same hurt-little-girl expression.

"I'm not being my mother. I am just being practical. If he hurts an elbow or a joint at this age, wait 'til you see the bills then! And that'll nix his show debut," she adds defensively.

Gus relents. "Just let him be, OK?" He pulls into the Burger King drive-up window.

Rufus is aroused by the fast food aromas. He pushes his huge head between the front bucket seats and drools exuberantly, as Gus orders through the intercom: "A quarter pounder for me, a veggie burger for her, and a quarter pounder for him" – he gestures at the slobbering giant – "no roll."

Still miffed, Maria is feeling contrary. "Is this a good idea? We don't want to feed him junk food. We have to watch his weight."

Gus ignores her as he reaches out the window to take the proffered bag. He takes the veggie burger out and hands it to Maria. He sets the bag down on the console between the front seats and pulls his own burger out.

"Why don't we ask him?" Gus teases. Rufus, not waiting for his cue, puts his head into the bag and inhales the remaining burger. Maria shakes her head in disapproval. Unfazed, Rufus smacks his lips and belches loudly. Neither Maria nor Gus can suppress a chuckle.

Chapter Fourteen

Five weeks more of the Wednesday night obedience class and Burger King routine and the five puppies are assembled in the Bath gym for graduation. Patty has the handlers sit their puppies in a circle. She calls out each dog to receive a certificate and a bag of treats.

Largest is last. Rufus' turn is next. While Patty is awarding Chloe, the Labrador, her diploma, Maria whips out a child's mortarboard and fastens it on Rufus' head. When his name is called, Rufus trots proudly to the center, Gus in tow.

"Ah, the Graduate," Patty quips. Rufus shakes his head, freeing himself of his cap and begs a treat. Gus beams proudly while Maria clicks a picture.

Patty initiates a round of applause. "Well done, everybody. So we'll see you all in two weeks for the advanced obedience and show handling class. Have a good break and keep practicing."

✻✻✻

In the two-week interval Rufus, the perfect pupil, has somehow morphed into Rufus, the brat. For one thing at nine months he is bigger still, standing almost his full twenty-eight inches and already weighing one hundred-twenty pounds, and he has become full of himself. He tests Gus' and Maria's patience and asserts his Newfie stubborn streak.

For no apparent reason on this back-to-class night, Rufus is refusing to enter the Bath gym. He has gone on strike in the hallway, lying down and pretending to be glued to the cool linoleum.

Gus is clearly annoyed. "Come on, Rufus, let's go," he says sternly, as he tugs on the leash. Rufus responds by putting his head on his paws and giving Gus a mournful, but intransigent look.

Maria tries the opposite tack. She takes out a treat and cajoles, "Come on, Rufie. Mommy's got a cookie."

Rufus, who is rarely one to miss a tasty morsel, ignores her. Maria backs down the hallway, squats, and tries again to entice him. "Rufus, come. Homemade peanut butter cookie." Clearly, no amount of coaxing is going to budge Rufus.

After a long day of managing investments in a volatile market, Gus is in no mood to be embarrassed by a dog. He loses his temper. "God damn it! Let's go!" Impatiently tugging on the lead, Gus drags Rufus across the polished floor.

Maria looks upset; she, too, is embarrassed, but more by her husband than the dog. She follows Gus and Rufus to join the circle of other dogs and handlers.

The new teacher, Denise, is a petite, mousy, businesslike trainer, whose breed is the miniature poodle. Handling in the toy group gives her a supercilious sense of professional control. She, herself, could not do better with Rufus, but that does not prevent her from shooting Gus and Maria a glance of barely concealed disapproval. Maria lowers her eyes, but Gus stares back, still seething. "Not an auspicious start," Maria thinks.

Denise clears her throat and recovers her schoolmarm persona. "OK, so we are going to begin with walking around the ring using your show lead. Dog on your left. Lead up short; brisk pace; make sure your dog heels."

The other dogs fall into place eagerly and trot off. Bringing up the rear with Gus, Rufus balks, nips at the lead, and does his very best to botch the exercise. Gus soldiers through and pulls Rufus up next to Maria, who has been anxiously watching. Making no effort to conceal his annoyance, Gus tells her, "This isn't working. You try!"

Denise comes over and correctly positions Rufus at Maria's left and shows her how to hold the lead. She whispers some suggestions to which Maria nods politely. "OK," Denise urges. "Let's try again. Just Rufus."

This time Rufus takes off at such a gallop that Maria stumbles, loses the lead and falls. Ignoring his wife, Gus corrals the errant beast.

"I think that's it for tonight!" he bellows. Dragging Rufus by the collar, he heads over to the bleachers to pack up their belongings. Silently, he and Maria put on their coats and begin to leave.

Denise intercepts their flight. "Mr. and Mrs. Sundergaard, may I speak to you for a moment?" Like two children being reprimanded by their schoolmarm, Gus and Maria stand crestfallen before Denise. "I'm not sure what is going on with Rufus," she continues in a patronizing tone. "Whether he is just being a teenaged boy or he is not show material, but I think you ought to rethink his placement in this class. Perhaps there is another activity he might enjoy more. I'll give you some time to consider it and call you during the week, if I may?"

Maria is fighting back tears. Gus is simply enraged at everyone and everything. Without a reply, Gus and Maria head for the door. This time Rufus needs no encouragement. He races out of the gym, dragging Maria behind him.

Gus loads Rufus into the back of the van and slams the car door. He and Maria get in front, but Gus does not start the car. He sits there, hands gripping the wheel, seething. Maria tries a little wit to alleviate the moment. "We should have named him Bartleby, instead. *I prefer not to* seems to be his mantra," she quips wryly. She is not prepared for the full blast of Gus' anger.

"This whole dog thing is a goddamn disaster!" he shouts. "I'm too old for this. I don't enjoy being embarrassed by a four-legged brat!"

"Gus, please. We need a little patience."

"Well, I'm not going to take him back there. You can take him yourself if you want."

"We can't just give up like that," Maria pleads.

"We're not giving up. We're just refusing to waste our time."

"You want Rufus to be perfect, and if he's not, then you make an excuse or quit!" YOU sound like my mother now." The words escape Maria's lips before she can stop herself.

"Leave your mother out of this, Maria."

"Why should I? You know it's true. You know how many times she did the same thing to me. Over and over again, my whole life!"

Maria is unraveling now. Only the torrent of her words surpresses the impending sobs. "I loved my horseback riding lessons. But one day, I fell off. I wasn't even hurt. I got right back on. But she wouldn't let me ride anymore. She told the instructor I had "soft bones" and it was too dangerous! Or my ballet lessons when I was five! After the first recital when she saw how much better my friend Joy danced, she pulled me from the class. She told the teacher I had "fallen arches." The truth was that I hadn't met her expectations."

By now she is breathless. She hisses: "Mother's motto: all or nothing! No in-between! No learning curve! We can't just give up on Rufie like that. You and I are not going to do that! If he were our child, we wouldn't just quit."

"Well, he's not our child," Gus yells. "He's a bloody dog!"

The interruption stops Maria cold. She realizes the argument is about to derail into a full-fledged brawl. She takes a deep breath and switches gears, trying to initiate a compromise. "He's a teenaged puppy. He is just feeling his oats a little. Maybe we could try a different class or get a professional handler."

Gus is not to be deterred. "This show business is fucking bullshit! I told you I didn't want any part of it. Let him be a plain old pet, for Christ's sake!"

"But, Gus, we said we'd try."

He cuts her off. "I am not going through what I did all those years with the cats. We've been there, done that!"

Speechless, Maria stares hard at Gus and for an instant sees Nils Sundergaard instead. She feels suddenly helpless and panicky, the way she felt so often in those difficult years.

Chapter Fifteen

Madison Square Garden is abuzz with all the excitement of the Miss America Pageant, except that the contestants on this particular Saturday in 2003 are felines. High above the shoulder-to-shoulder crowded hall a banner proclaims the premiere annual event in the cat fancy: CFA International Cat Show.

On the floor below, threading their way through the teeming aisles is the local network television crew. They weave in and out among the spectators, pausing periodically to film a cat and its owner. The Persian ladies primp their fluffy charges. The Bengal owners stroke their kitties' sleek spotted fur with chamois as if buffing an expensive automobile. The Siamese handlers wear the bat-eared, blue-eyed, pointed creatures like boas around their necks, and the Maine Coon breeders lift their twenty-pound lynx-like creatures, stretched out high in the air to show off their long, muscular bodies.

On the opposite side of the hall, the six judging rings all have competitions in progress. The few rows of seats are all occupied, and standees crowd around, making it difficult for the contestants to fight their way to the ring. Though there is no monetary prize, Best in Show is still the coveted distinction of each owner or breeder.

Maria Sundergaard is no exception. She is seated in Ring One watching Judge Louise Lefebre award her Allbreed final. Lefebre, a buxom woman with a French Canadian accent, makes the presentation high drama. She is elegantly coiffed, wearing a glittery gown, bedecked with oodles of cat themed jewelry. She has already taken seven of the ten finalists out of their cages, held them up for the audience to ooh and ahh and the press to snap their pictures, and awarded them each a rosette.

As she puts the fourth place Himalayan back, Maria begins to bite her nails nervously. She leans over to a breeder colleague sitting beside her and whispers, "Oh, I'm a wreck! I wish my husband were here." She breathes a little sigh of relief as the Bengal wins third place. This means her cat is second or best!

"And now, may I have the owners of cat #130, the Maine Coon, and cat #152, the Persian," Lefebre commands. Maria and her rival stand alongside the judge's table.

"Please take your cats out and present them to our audience," Lefebre instructs. The two women oblige, holding their felines aloft for the cameras. Lefebre asks the Persian owner to reveal her cat's name and age. "Cee's Delight. She's two" is the reply. The judge praises the cat's cobby body, beautiful eye color, fabulous coat and presentation. She then turns to Maria.

"*And your cat's name and age?*"

"*Mannahatta's Skrimshander, and he is three years old," Maria says proudly.*

Lefebre tells the crowd: "A beautiful specimen of a Maine Coon: long rectangular body, great boning, square muzzle, beautiful ear set, gorgeous smoke color, and a real showman!"

Making the most drama of the moment, Lefebre steps back and studies the two cats. She looks at the audience to build suspense. "Both are beautiful examples of their breeds, but this is how I see it today. My second best cat..." She pauses with exaggeration before handing the rosette to the Persian owner. "And my Best in Show is my Maine Coon!" Lefebre takes Skrimshander from Maria's arms, holds him up high above her head, and sets him down on the table, draping the rosette on the cat's shoulders.

Maria blurts out ecstatically, "Oh, my God, that makes him a Supreme Grand Champion!" As if on cue, Skrimshander extends his large, tufted paws and pumps them vigorously in a prayerful gesture, a gracious thank you to his admirers. The audience goes wild.

Chapter Sixteen

An hour later after fighting the 5:00 p.m. maze of Lincoln Tunnel traffic, Maria pulls into her North Bergen driveway. She enters the house by the front doorway, setting down Skrimshander in his carrier.

"Gus, I'm home," she calls out, delight in her voice. "I'm home. We had a great show!" She lets Skrimshander out of his carrier and walks through the rooms looking for Gus. At the bottom of the stairwell she calls upstairs. "Gus are you up there?" With no reply, she opens the French doors to the kitchen. Immediately, she spots a note on the table. "He must have gone somewhere," she thinks. She picks up the paper with her husband's distinctive, all capital letter scrawl.

"IT'S ME OR THE CATS."

Maria's heart skips a beat. She races for the phone and starts dialing Gus' cell. Ring after ring until it goes into voicemail. She panics and tries the number over and over before finally giving up. Helplessly, she collapses at the kitchen table, head in arms and sobs desolately.

✳✳✳

The clock on the wall strikes 10:00 p.m. Maria has succumbed to her despair and exhaustion. Something rouses her. She wipes her eyes and glances at the time. Almost mechanically, she reaches for the phone and dials Gus again. This time she leaves a message. "Gus, please, where are you? I am so worried. Please, please come home. We'll work it out. I'll do whatever we need to work it out."

The back door opens softly, and a subdued Gus enters. His shoulders slump wearily, and his face is drained. Maria drops the phone and runs to him, hugging him hard.

"Oh, Gus, Gus, don't ever leave me again. Please don't. We promised to be there for each other always no matter what. And we have been for thirty-three years. I love you so much!"

In a depressed monotone, Gus concedes, "I love you, too, but sometimes it's all too much."

"What is? What is too much?" Maria checks herself in terror as she remembers the suicide attempt two years ago. "Oh, my God, Gus, please! No!"

Chapter Seventeen

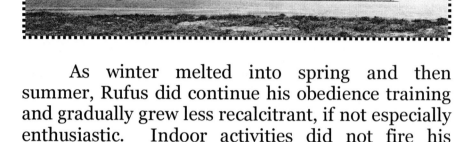

As winter melted into spring and then summer, Rufus did continue his obedience training and gradually grew less recalcitrant, if not especially enthusiastic. Indoor activities did not fire his interest. Rather than trotting on a show lead, he loved running in the woods or gamboling on a beach.

At every opportunity Gus and Maria do take Rufus to one of their favorite ocean spots. On this particular warm sunny June day, the three are padding along the strand at Reid State Park, letting the cool blue waves caress their toes.

A little distance down the otherwise deserted beach, two small children are playing in the surf. Their parents are seated on a blanket, keeping a watchful eye. Suddenly, Rufus rivets his focus on the youngsters. He is fascinated by their splashing. Gus recognizes the look in the dog's eye.

"STAY, Rufus," he quickly commands, but Rufus ignores the order, races a few yards down the beach, and plunges into the water. He swims effortlessly out to the children and begins circling them repeatedly, driving them closer and closer to shore.

Maria gasps: "Gus, look, he's swimming!"

Sharing her wonder, Gus replies, "He's rescuing them. That's what they do when they want to bring a swimmer in."

The children's father calls his charges back. "Brie, Joey, come in now."

Giggling, fascinated by the big bear-dog, the children splash their way to shore. Rufus continues to swim protectively alongside them. Once on the beach, Rufus shakes himself off and parks himself in a SIT at Gus and Maria's feet. He is obviously proud of his "rescue." Maria and Gus give him hugs while Brie and Joey watch enthralled.

"You can pet him, if you want," Maria gently tells the children. Brie and Joey reach down and tentatively pat the huge head, and then squeal with pleasure.

Gus smiles at the towheaded kids. "You remind me of me when I was your age," he says nostalgically, ruffling Joey's hair. He grins again at the children and their parents and turns out to the horizon.

❋❋❋

A flaxen-haired five-year-old Gösta Sundergaard is romping in the rough Cape Cod surf at Wellfleet. A feisty little Boston terrier is trying to keep up with his fearless companion, who ventures further and further into the waves. Snapping at the white caps wildly, Timmy keeps getting pushed back to shore. His yelps alert Nils and Vilma, sitting on the dunes.

Nils stand and motions boy and dog to come in. Unlike young Maria, little Gus giggles mischievously and defies his parents. He wades out farther, splashing gaily. Nils does not like his authority brooked, even in jest. He marches sternly to the water's edge, collars Timmy, and shouts: "Get in here this minute, young man!"

Gus ends the game and trots out, his lips set defiantly.

~~~~~~

"What are you dreaming about?" Maria asks Gus.

"Cape Cod," he replies.

"Oh, the Cape. We have to go next summer. We haven't been in a while now ever since we began to plan for Maine," Maria posits.

They call Rufus to follow and continue down the beach, reminiscing.

"Remember our honeymoon?" Gus asks. "You wanted to camp on the dunes in October, and I wanted to know if you were crazy."

"Well, we had no money, and it was a romantic idea. O'Neill and Agnes did it. They lived in a shack out there," Maria recalls.

"Remember O'Neill's doctor," Gus asks. "What was his name? Dr. Hiebert?"

"Yeah," Maria smiles. "It was our first summer vacation together in Truro. That huge bee had stung me earlier in the day, and you put ice on it. We went to dinner at Ciro and Sal's, and as we were walking down the street in Ptown, I blew up like a balloon and passed out."

"A shopkeeper called an ambulance, and they rushed you to Hiebert's clinic, passing the stretcher through the window because it wouldn't make the turn on the old porch," Gus fills in.

"And I woke up at that very moment and hit my head on the window! And poor Dr. Hiebert cleared the waiting room of the druggies getting their B-12 shots and the bleeding fishermen and immediately gave me an adrenalin shot."

"My God, that was close!" Gus remembers soberly. "And then he came back to our cottage at 1:00 a.m. to check on you. And charged us $25 for the whole deal!"

Maria laughs. "Well, it was 1972! But, yeah, they don't make them like that anymore – that kind of dedication." They have reached the path through the tall grasses leading back to their car. "Let's sit a minute, hon." They plop themselves down with Rufus beside them.

"Do you remember what I said to you that day before I lost consciousness," Maria says softly. "We had just seen *Love Story*, and I was sure I was dying."

"I do," Gus whispers. He slips his arm around her shoulders and whispers in her ear, "I love you, and I will love you forever," he quotes.

"Me, too," she adds bringing the conversation into the present, "now and always."

Chapter Eighteen

A week later on a splendid summer Saturday, Gus, Maria, and Rufus have driven to Camden. They hike Mt. Battie, Rufus surprisingly game for the trek, and act like tourists as they pose for pictures in front of the stunning panorama.

After the morning's exertions, the trio parks itself on a bench overlooking the harbor. Rufus is leashed and sits peaceably while Gus and Maria bask in the sun, behind them the classical perfection of the Frederick Olmsted manicured gardens and quintessential New England cupola adorned brick library building. Stretching before them, the harbor is filled with schooners, windjammers, and sailboats. The crested ducks swim above in the falls, and their mallard cousins frolic in the harbor waters below. The gulls swoop down for mussels left by fishermen. It is a snapshot of complete harmony.

Gus marvels, "It's just like a postcard, isn't it? Sometimes, I have to pinch myself to believe we really LIVE in Maine now. I don't have to pack up and go home after summer vacation."

"It's the water," Maria suggests, "so much of it everywhere, stretching out to the sky."

"How did we live all those years?" Gus asks. "I keep asking myself how did I fight the traffic into

Manhattan day after day? And the crowds and the noise and the pollution and – "

"And the stress," Maria finishes his sentence.

"And the stress," Gus agrees. "You know I still feel as if I am just learning to unwind." Glancing at the bevy of boats in the harbor, he switches to a more upbeat mode. "I can't wait to get my boat," he says, indicating a modest sailboat. "I'm going to take Rufus with me to explore the coast. He'll be my First Mate. Would you like that, Rufie?"

He studies Rufus who ignores Gus and is zeroing in on the harbor action. Gus continues, "Look at him! He just loves the water, doesn't he? He could sit here all day."

"So could I," Maria adds.

"No, I mean the sea is his home. If I were to let him off this leash, he'd be in there in a heartbeat."

"Yeah, he really does love the water. No coaxing needed," Maria agrees.

Suddenly, Gus becomes animated. "Let's do it!"

"Do what?" Maria asks.

"Let's forget the show dog thing and train him for water rescue. His heart is in it." He takes his wife's hand and adds, "And so is mine."

Without hesitation, Maria replies, "Then let's do it!"

Chapter Nineteen

Whenever Gus and Maria made up their minds to do something, they forged ahead with limitless enthusiasm. Not more than one week after their Camden epiphany, Maria had found a water rescue trainer; Gus had purchased life jackets, a wet suit, bumpers, a life preserver – all the training gear.

Early on the following Sunday morning, Gus, Maria, and Rufus leave Brunswick at dawn and drive northwest to Moosehead Lake. They pause downtown to pick up two lattes and some sinfully delicious apple turnovers at Wild Oats. Then electing the scenic route, they head to Greenville.

When they arrive at 10:00 a.m., Penny Horne is already there. She has set up the markers, beached the rowboat, and set down a basket of rescue props.

The tall, blonde Nordic woman with high cheekbones and steel-blue eyes is lean and athletic. An airline pilot in her former career, she now breeds Newfs and Maine Coons, serendipity that immediately endears her to Maria. Penny's voice has the no-nonsense neutrality and resolve of a professional who can safely land a jet on one engine, but her aura is that of an earth goddess – warm, caring, bountiful. They greet as if long-lost friends.

Penny spends a few minutes playing with Rufus and then explains the routine for the water test to Gus and Maria. "They are usually naturals, so don't sweat it," she assures Rufus' nervous parents. "However, even my Pocahontas who is WDX refused to do the exercises she knew in her sleep at the last Newf Fun Day Demo. That's a Newf for you! Anyway, let's keep it fun for him, as well."

For several hours Penny puts Rufus through the basic paces. Gus and Maria watch in awe. When they break for the gourmet lunch, which Penny has provided, despite the Sundergaards' protests that they should take her out to eat, the trio (or quartet with Rufus) relaxes together on the banks of the huge, primeval lake.

Driving back in the early afternoon, Gus, Maria, and Rufus, who is snoring in his crate, all have a huge sense of fulfillment. For six weeks, they repeat the ritual, and finally in late summer they meet Penny to run a rehearsal for the September water trials.

As usual, Penny has everything set up for Gus, Maria, and Rufus' arrival. She greets them warmly and gives Rufus a big hug. The dog responds with a slobbery kiss.

"OK, let's go through the whole sequence from the beginning, no stopping, if possible," Penny says. "Gus, you row out to the twenty-five-foot marker and take the extra life jacket. Maria, you can cheer us on, and I'll handle him from shore." The dog seems impatient to get started. He is all eagerness and energy.

When Gus reaches his marker in the rowboat, Penny puts the dog into a correct SIT/STAY facing the lake. She then throws the yellow bumper with a line attached far out into the lake and commands Rufus to retrieve it. Without a second's pause, the big bear-dog wades into the water and swims directly to his target with powerful, muscular strokes. Like Mark Spitz doing the free style, Rufus reaches out with his left and then right legs to churn through the water. He takes the bumper in his mouth, circles round, and powers back to shore, delivering it to Penny's hand.

Handler and dog again face the lake, ready for the second test. Gus drops the life jacket from the boat into the water. Penny hand-signals to Rufus that he is to fetch the jacket. Again, the dog slices through the water to the floating life jacket; he takes the straps in this mouth and swims back to Penny, plunking his trophy into her hand. He circles once and vigorously shakes off water from his heavy, oily outer coat and then plants himself to Penny's left, waiting for the next cue.

Gus has jumped off the anchored boat and has swum out to the fifty-foot marker. He begins to splash wildly, feigning drowning. He calls loudly, "Rufus, help! Help!"

The dog leans forward in his SIT/STAY, ready to plunge in. Penny signals Rufus to grasp in his teeth a heavy rope fastened to a life preserver and immediately gives the hand signal for Rufus to "rescue" the victim. Rufus accelerates through the water, reaching Gus in only a few seconds more than it took him to complete the earlier exercises. The dog circles Gus so that his human can grasp the life preserver. Once he is sure that he has his man in tow, Rufus pulls with the horsepower of a diesel engine until Gus is dragged up onto the beach.

Man and dog shake themselves, but there is no time for celebration. Rufus knows he has not yet completed his tasks. He sits patiently at Penny's side as Gus swims back out to the boat and clambers in using the special flat platform on the stern. Penny waits until Gus is settled and then makes Rufus take a bumper with a longer line attached and directs him out to the boat again. Rufus races toward his goal. Gus reaches down, catches the end of the line, and lashes it tight to the boat.

"Pull us in, Ruf," he commands. Without hesitation, bumper still in jaws, the massive dog hauls the rowboat and man toward shore, beaching the craft in the sandy shallows.

This time Penny takes the oars while Gus and Rufus climb onto the stern platform facing away from her. Penny rows nimbly and briskly out to the fifty-foot marker. She positions the boat for this last, most crucial test.

Gus impersonates a man overboard, tumbling off the platform into the deep water. He begins splashing with the intensity of someone drowning, shouting, "Help! Help!"

Penny signals Rufus to dive in. Surprisingly, the dog checks for a moment, seeming uncertain how to get his one hundred-fifty-pound frame into the water from the stern platform. Gus doubles his splashy panic. Penny seems taken aback that Rufus has failed to respond. She signals again more imperatively. "Go, Ruf, go! Now!"

Suddenly, her meaning registers in Rufus' memory. He springs off his hind legs – back arched, front legs extended full out – and dives dramatically into the lake. In two strokes he reaches Gus' side and clamps his jaws onto Gus' forearm. Gus rolls over onto his back and goes limp, letting his life jacket support him as Rufus pulls him in.

Maria is shouting encouragement as Rufus nears completion of the trial. "That's it, boy! Come on, Rufus!"

Making up for his moment of indecision, Rufus quickens his pace and deposits Gus at Maria's feet, just barely within the allotted time. He performs the obligatory SIT to end the sequence, but though his hindquarters are planted on the sand, he is all animation. His eyes are flashing, his tail is flailing, and his big tongue hangs out in a slobbery display of Newfie pride.

Penny has rowed in, beaches the boat, and jumps out. She greets her pupils enthusiastically. "Practically perfect! He has to make that dive faster or he'll be disqualified, but other than that, he was great!"

Maria hands Gus a towel. Instead of using it for himself, he bends down to dry his dog. Rufus rewards the solicitude with a big, sloppy kiss on the lips.

"Good boy! You were amazing!" Maria beams. "Now he just has to do same thing on the test next week."

"And if he does," Gus promises, "We're going to put in that pool."

Thinking of the cost, Maria starts to protest, "Well, we'll see."

Gus engages her eyes with his firm smile. "This dog," he vows, "is going to change my life!"

Chapter Twenty

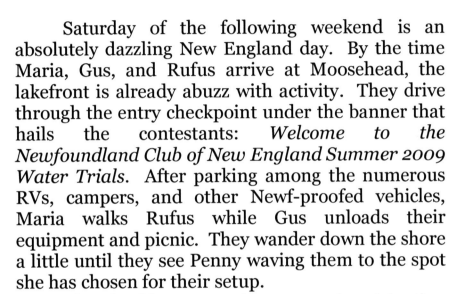

Saturday of the following weekend is an absolutely dazzling New England day. By the time Maria, Gus, and Rufus arrive at Moosehead, the lakefront is already abuzz with activity. They drive through the entry checkpoint under the banner that hails the contestants: *Welcome to the Newfoundland Club of New England Summer 2009 Water Trials*. After parking among the numerous RVs, campers, and other Newf-proofed vehicles, Maria walks Rufus while Gus unloads their equipment and picnic. They wander down the shore a little until they see Penny waving them to the spot she has chosen for their setup.

The air of intense excitement and anticipation among the participants, human and canine, makes the gathering feel more like a race at Saratoga than the annual working dog water competition. The two judges are already seated under a canopy close to the water's edge; they are carefully reviewing the catalog of entries and readying their scorecards. The stewards have donned their life jackets and lined up on the shore. The beached rowboats are ready to go. The loudspeaker calls the first few dogs' numbers. Handlers and Newfoundlands line up at the waterfront.

Meanwhile, Gus has erected the shade canopy under which Rufus now sits, tongue hanging out, taking in all the action. Gus opens the Harrod's picnic basket, a gift to themselves which he and Maria had bought many years ago in London. From years of practice at Tanglewood and Ravinia, Gus lays out the tartan cloth and the elegant picnic ware. In lieu of wine in the stemware, he pours himself, Maria, and, yes, Rufus, some water. He puts on his life jacket and water shoes as Maria strains to hear the call and nervously leafs through the catalog.

"Dog number 25, please."

"That's it," Maria announces to Gus. "We're next. Can he do it?" she asks Penny.

"We'll see," Penny replies matter-of-factly. "Let's go."

All four walk down to the shore and take their positions. Dog number 25 is finishing the last exercise. A steward approaches Penny, checking his entry list.

"So this is Midship's Sea Dog Rufus? Are you ready?" Penny nods calmly. Gus just sets his jaw firmly. "You may begin," the steward tells them.

With Rufus sitting at her side, Penny tosses the bumper twenty-five feet out and signals her charge to go. For Maria, standing a few feet back, the familiar sequence seems to take place in slow, fluid motion, each step elongated by the tension, gravity, and exquisite beauty of the dog.

As if driven by an ancient, noble instinct, Rufus propels through the water like a tremendous machine, focused single-mindedly on his task. A star athlete, the huge dog has the stamina and grace of Secretariat, the heart of Rocky Balboa, and the balletic lyricism of Baryshnikov. He is loving every minute of his chance to prove himself, to do what he was born to do!

He streaks through the pond, bumper in mouth and confidently returns the prop directly to Penny's hand. To Maria's eyes, one task seems to blend seamlessly into the next. By the time she catches her breath after the first exercise, she sees that the two stewards have already positioned the row-boat out in the lake and have dropped the life jacket into the water. Penny has sent Rufus out, and the dog is now effortlessly gliding back to shore with the jacket in his teeth. Having perfectly transferred it to Penny's hand, he stands up in the shallows, shakes himself off, and looks eagerly at his handler for the next cue.

At fifty feet out, the first steward is in the water, splashing loudly and yelling, "Help, Rufus, help!" The sounds are like adrenalin to Rufus. He immediately takes the rope with the life preserver attached that Penny proffers and powers out to the "drowning man," circling him. As soon as the steward grabs the life preserver, Rufus makes a sweeping arc and heads for shore. Dog and man weigh the same, but in the Newfoundland's safekeeping, the steward seems weightless.

Maria, who hasn't taken her eyes off Rufus, suddenly realizes that Gus is no longer standing beside Penny. He has rowed the second boat out fifty-feet, waiting for Penny to send Rufus to him with the bumper and line.

The dog, responding to Penny's command but energized by seeing Gus on the lake, strengthens his focus. He knows his mission is to bring man and boat quickly to safety. Scarcely has Gus reached down for the line and fastened it to the boat, than Rufus is masterfully breast-stroking to shore. Dog and boat create a tremendous wake.

Maria is cheering, though she cannot hear herself. She has somehow stepped outside her body; so in tune is she with her beloved competitors that she, too, is on the lake.

Back on shore, Gus has no time to acknowledge her. With a quick pat on Rufus' head, he bids his Newf to sit beside him on the rear platform of the boat. After launching the boat into the shallows, the two stewards climb aboard and row their passengers to the marker. Rufus sits proudly erect beside Gus, who has his arm looped loosely around the dog's neck. The dog's eyes are fixed on the rippling water.

When the stewards have settled the boat, Gus takes their cue and pretends to fall off the platform into the water. He is just beginning to splash when a searing heaviness shoots up his left arm and across his chest.

"Go, Rufus, go!" Maria chants from the shore. This is the moment of uncertainty.

Gus' right hand flies to his breast as he lets out a strangled cry. The splashing stops as Gus falls face forward into the water. Only his life jacket keeps him afloat.

His cry shakes Maria from her disembodied state. A look of panic and horror crosses her face as a whispered plea escapes her lips. "Gus, Gus! Oh, my God, Gus, what's wrong? Oh, God, no!"

At almost the same instant that Gus has gone motionless, Rufus rallies. Without a jot of hesitation, without prompting from the steward or signals from Penny, he catapults himself off the boat and, with an economy of stride, reaches his beloved Gus. He dives under his victim and uses his massive head to roll Gus over onto his back. His soft, but powerful mouth closes firmly on Gus' arm. He hears Maria's cries of "Help! Help! Get a doctor! Rufus, swim, Rufus!" But the dog needs no urging. Realizing his life-and-death mission, Rufus rushes through the water to the beach. Within the few minutes it takes to lay Gus at Maria's feet, the entire lakefront has erupted into emergency mode. One steward dials 911, as his colleague rows furiously to shore. People run from all directions to meet Rufus. Spectators leave their picnics and crowd around.

A man pushes through the throng to the place where Rufus, Maria, and Penny kneel, silent sentinels around Gus.

"I'm a doctor. Everyone stand back!" He immediately removes Gus' life jacket and starts vigorous CPR. Screams in the distance of the

approaching ambulance inject a shrill counterpoint
to the doctor's pumping and pounding.

Chapter Twenty-One

It seems an eternity to Maria, but within minutes she is climbing into the ambulance and kneeling down beside Gus' gurney. A paramedic has already hooked his patient up to the defibrillator and is monitoring him closely. Tears streaming down her face, Maria searches the young technician's face for clues. Her eyes go back and forth between the monitor, where the squiggle of Gus' heartbeat moves up and down irregularly across the screen, and the noncommittal concentration of the emergency worker. Then, as the ambulance, lights flashing, careens up to the hospital Emergency Room entrance, Gus flutters his eyelids. Maria sucks in her breath in relief and reaches for his hand. With practiced haste, the paramedics rush Gus' gurney into the ER, Maria hurrying after them.

✳✳✳

Several hours have ticked by as Maria sits alone in the monastic austerity of the waiting room outside the Cardiovascular Surgery Unit. Anxiously, she bites her nails to the quick and compulsively checks her watch, comparing it to the huge wall clock, whose ticking sounds like Big Ben in the anxious stillness of the room.

Maria is living her worst nightmare: that inescapable day which has haunted her for seventeen years. She remembers her panic when Gus suffered his first heart attack. She had called his office, and his secretary had told her that Mr. Sundergaard had not come in to work. Like an elevator gone wild, her heart plunged! "My, God!" she cried. "Help me find him! Call the police, the hospitals!"

The secretary had politely put her on hold and gotten Gus' boss, Warren Smythe, who managed to calm Maria and promised assistance. Within minutes he had called back to say Gus was in the Emergency Room of Englewood Hospital with chest pains.

"Oh, God, a heart attack!" Maria blurted out.

"Maybe, but not a major one. He's OK; he's conscious," Smythe reassured Maria. "What can we do for you?"

✳✳✳

The next few weeks had been unsettling. Gus had, indeed, suffered a minor heart attack; angioplasty had not proved successful, but he was pronounced stable on medication and a regimen of diet and exercise.

Gus came home a soberer and angrier man. His father, Nils, had died of a massive coronary only four months before. His brother, Anselm, had had bypass surgery only one month ago, and now he, Gus, had been afflicted with the Sundergaard scourge. At forty-five years old, he faced the chilling reality of his own mortality.

And from that moment on, Maria lived in a state of dread. They bought cell phones. Gus called Maria each morning when he arrived at work and minutes before he left. When he traveled for business, they set three times a day to touch base; sometimes, when a hotel phone went momentarily unanswered, Maria considered calling the desk to check on him.

And, yet, as the years passed, Gus, a responsible patient, grew leaner and fitter, improved his cholesterol, changed his diet, and experienced fewer bouts of angina. He and Maria lulled themselves into denial. The terrifying infirmity harbored in Gus' genes could be kept at bay.

"Especially now," Maria thought, "when their new life had just begun."

✳✳✳

"You OK?" A voice jolts Maria out of her contemplation. Looking up, she sees Penny, who sits down next to her friend and hands her a coffee.

"Not really."

Penny slips an arm around Maria's shoulders. "Drink it. You're still in shock. It all happened so fast."

Seeing Penny reminds Maria. "Rufus? Where's Rufus?"

"He's fine. John took him home to our place."

Relief overwhelms Maria. "Thank God! Thank God for Rufus," she mumbles, dissolving into sobs.

Chapter Twenty-Two

The sun filtered through the lace curtains in the Sundergaard bedroom bathes Gus in comforting warmth. He is sitting up in bed one week after his surgery, reading the *Wall Street Journal*. Rufus pads into the room and puts his big head on the mattress, his soulful brown eyes querying Gus' face.

Gus pats the bed encouraging the dog to jump up. Rufus, aware that this is an unusual privilege, immediately obliges, lying down next to Gus, his head on Maria's pillow. He drools happily.

Maria does a double take when she brings in the breakfast tray. "Hey, Rufie, that's my spot. Don't get used to it."

Gus teases, "And why not? No worse than a bunch of cats!"

Maria sets the tray on Gus' lap and looks for some room to perch herself. Gus samples the juice and yogurt. It is clearly not the breakfast he had in mind.

"What diet is this?"

"The one the doctor ordered."

"I don't need to lose weight," he sulks.

"No, you've already done that."

"And I look nineteen again!"

"You look frail," his wife's small, worried voice ventures. Then, turning upbeat, she adds, "But that is neither here nor there. It has only been seven days. The doctor says you'll be fine in another couple weeks if you do what he says, and I'm here to make sure you do."

"And I have no say?"

"Not right now anyway," Maria replies firmly.

"What do you say, Rufus?" Gus deflects.

"He wants you completely well so we can be a family again."

"We are a family, aren't we?" Gus corrects.

"Yes," she whispers, "but I think we always have been."

"Maybe you knew that," he concedes, "but I didn't."

"That's not true, Gus. You could have chosen differently. You didn't."

Gus seems perplexed. "What?"

Maria hesitates for a moment. She considers backing down but then continues softly, "This isn't the time. We can talk about it when you're all better.'

"No, what?"

"No, really." She kisses his forehead, trying to dismiss the painful memory.

He persists. "What are you saying?"

Sighing, Maria opens the Pandora's box. "You left after that cat show. And you thought of leaving again. You went to James Blythe the next year to talk about a divorce. He told you he couldn't represent you because he was OUR lawyer. He gave you a referral."

Gus is taken aback. "How do you know that?"

"James told me afterwards when I went to him to close Uncle John's estate. He was happy for us that we had moved on together. It was simple disclosure."

"But I never – " Gus breaks off.

"It doesn't matter now," Maria soothes. "It didn't happen. We stayed."

"But I never," her husband continues to protest as much to himself as to her.

"Gus, it's OK. You're alive! We're here in Maine. We've got our wonderful dream home. We live in the most beautiful place in the world. We've got our furry family, especially Rufus." The dog, hearing his name, lifts his head, yawns, and settles back down on the pillow.

Maria continues the pep talk. "We have friends. You've got only three more years to work from home, and we are as happy as we have ever been in forty years. We've got each other. All that is behind us. That's why we came here – to leave that all behind."

Softly, Gus contradicts," It's never wholly behind us." His words conjure up the long suppressed torment.

Their neat white house and secluded patio. Gus slumped over on the wrought iron bench, sobbing helplessly. Maria, the belt-noose in her trembling hands, falling on her knees beside her husband and clutching him to her breast.

✳✳✳

"Gus, love, it's getting late," Maria coaxes. They are still sitting on the garden bench which is now bathed in a soft glow from the patio lights. Twilight gives the tiny brick enclave an urban serenity. "We can't sit here all night, hon. Let's go inside and have something to eat. I have your birthday present."

"Do you think I want it now?" Gus asks dully. "Do you think I can ever celebrate this day again? It's cursed, just as I am."

"Gus, you're just in shock. We all are, but please, try to focus on our blessings."

"Three thousand people died today," Gus erupts belligerently, "a mile away from here in full view of our windows! They held hands and jumped one hundred stories. They turned to ash before my very eyes!"

Maria throws her arms around him again. "I know, I know, but YOU didn't die. You are here in my arms."

"I could have. I was at Cantor Fitzgerald just last week for a meeting. We were going to meet again this week, but then Jack had a conflict."

Maria speaks slowly and firmly as if to a child. "But you DIDN'T," she says, trying to restore reality.

"Maybe I should have," Gus mutters morosely.

"Oh, no, no!" Maria is terrified. "Don't say that. You're alive because we've got lots of living to do. WE have lots of living. We'll get some professional help right away." She grabs his shoulder and forces Gus to look into her eyes. Intensely, she continues, "Because, Gösta Sundergaard, do you hear me?" She gives her husband a little shake. "We are going to grow old together. That's a promise!"

Gus shakes his head and pulls away, in his ice blue eyes a faraway, unreachable look.

"Why do you think you survived that first heart attack eight years ago? You could have died then. Look at your father!"

Gus deliberately meets Maria's gaze and says in a steely, quiet voice, "I killed him. I killed my father."

"What! Gus, you're raving!"

"I killed him." Gus breaks down hysterically. "I pulled the plug."

Chapter Twenty-Three

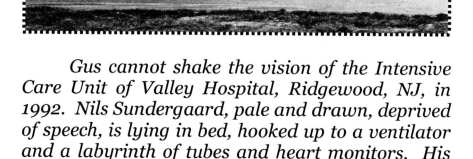

Gus cannot shake the vision of the Intensive Care Unit of Valley Hospital, Ridgewood, NJ, in 1992. Nils Sundergaard, pale and drawn, deprived of speech, is lying in bed, hooked up to a ventilator and a labyrinth of tubes and heart monitors. His wife, Vilma, and his children – Gus, Ingrid, Helmi, and Anselm – are assembled at the bedside. Vilma is holding Nils' hand, praying for a miracle.

The solemnity of the vigil is interrupted by the entrance of Dr. Kim. A young Asian cardiologist with an icy pragmatism and absolutely no bedside manner, he strides up to his patient. He checks the hospital chart, feels for pulse, and studies the monitors for a moment. Mentally dismissing the distraught Vilma, he chooses to address the sons.

"I'm afraid the news is not good. Your father has a hole in his heart that cannot be repaired. It is only a matter of time."

Anselm cuts Dr. Kim off. "Doctor, please, not here!"

Dr. Kim ignores him completely. "He can't hear us."

"But my mother and sisters can," Anselm insists with a fierce protectiveness.

"Well, perhaps they better listen," Dr. Kim continues coldly. "You all need to listen because I need a decision here. Mr. Sundergaard has no living will, so one of you here is going to have to decide what's next."

"Well, that should be Mother," Anselm declares. He gently helps Vilma to her feet and directs her tearful face toward the doctor. "Mother, the doctor wants to speak to you."

Dr. Kim takes a few steps toward Vilma, entering her space with an intimidating lack of empathy. "Mrs. Sundergaard, I can't help your husband," he declares matter-of-factly. "Surgery will not fix the hole in his heart. He has already lost consciousness. He has a few days or a few hours. In my opinion, the ventilator is too aggressive for his condition. It will just prolong the agony." Raising his voice for emphasis, he adds, " I need your permission to disconnect the ventilator. Mrs. Sundergaard?"

Vilma looks confused and is unable to answer.

"Mrs. Sundergaard?" Dr. Kim repeats sharply.

Robotically, Vilma replies, "It's not my decision. It's God's. God will do what is best for Nils." She looks around the room in a panic, searching her children's faces for a validation of her belief, but all four appear in shock. Ingrid and Helmi avert their eyes. Anselm directs his gaze nervously to the heart monitor, hoping for an answer from the device that, ironically, he, as an engineer, has helped design. Only Gus confronts Dr. Kim with a numb stare, which the doctor returns with an unyielding imperative one of his own.

Since no one is coming to her aid, Vilma falters: "Don't ask me. I can't choose! I am not God!" She appears ready to collapse. Anselm reaches around her waist and supports her into a chair.

"Dr. Kim," Anselm urges, "It's her blood pressure. She hasn't taken her medicine today. Can we get her some help?"

Without a word, Dr. Kim presses the button to summon a nurse, who arrives quickly with a wheelchair. She and Anselm help Vilma, who is close to fainting, into the chair and hurry her off to the Emergency Room.

Dr. Kim glances at his watch as if this latest drama has wasted some of his precious time. He surveys the remaining family. Ingrid and Helmi are on opposite sides of the bed, holding each of Nils' hands and weeping silently. Gus and Anselm stand at the foot of the bed, searching each other's eyes for direction.

With a tinge of sarcasm Dr. Kim demands, "Well, without your mother or God here to decide, who IS authorized to make this call?"

Grimly, Gus faces Dr. Kim. "I am. I have the Power of Attorney."

Taking a quick look at the chart to verify this, Kim thrusts a clipboard with paperwork at Gus. "Well, then, sign here."

Gus takes the pen and paper and slowly scans the document. He looks at Anselm one more time, hoping for support. His brother signals indecision. Gus pauses, his mind racing, and then signs the document authorizing the removal of life support. He drops the clipboard and pen on the bedside table, turns his back contemptuously on Dr. Kim, and joins his siblings in chairs at the bedside.

Not missing a beat, Dr. Kim disconnects the ventilator. So mechanically efficient is his movement that he does not pause to read the look of self-loathing that has spread over Gus' features.

✳✳✳

By the time Anselm wakes three hours later, he sees that, like himself, his brother and sisters have all dozed off. He blinks his eyes and checks the monitor, stands and walks around to rouse Gus. His brother's light tap on the shoulder causes Gus to start and instantly seek out the monitor. The line which had been fluttering feebly has now gone flat. Anselm snaps the monitor off and wakes his sisters as Gus glances at the bedside digital clock: 9/11/92 5:00 a.m.

Chapter Twenty-Four

"Oh, God, Gus, why didn't you ever tell me?" Maria asks softly, breaking the silence following her husband's revelation. They are still seated in the garden; night has fallen. Gus stares straight ahead; in the soft landscape lighting his face appears ghostly.

"Do you think I am proud of what I did?" he replies.

"But, Gus, it was the right thing. You had the POA. He had no living will. He would have suffered and died anyway!"

"That's not what my mother thought." Gus closes his eyes as he remembers.

✳✳✳

The November day is grim and gray as a hearse and two limousines file through the gates of George Washington Cemetery. The procession winds among the monotonous rows of plain granite headstones, stopping at the Sundergaard gravesite.

Solicitous, dark-suited figures open limousine doors and usher family members to the grave's edge. The priest nods kindly at Vilma, who is *leaning on Anselm's arm. Anselm's wife, Betsy, Helmi, Ingrid and her husband, Peter, huddle protectively around their mother. Gus stands a little apart, Maria's arm tucked through his. His face is almost livid with grief and stress, but in contrast to his siblings, he is dry-eyed. The priest drones the litany of burial: "We commit the body of your servant, Nils Sundergaard, to the grave in the hope of the resurrection. Dust to dust and ashes to ashes. May God's mercy shine upon him and grant him eternal life. In the name of the Father and the Son and the Holy Ghost. Amen."*

Gus is not listening, not to Father Stashu, not to Maria, who is whispering to him. "Gus, love, I'm here."

"Finally," Gus mutters bitterly.

"Gus, I came back the minute I heard."

"Yeah, how was the concert?"

"Gus, I drove all night. When we had talked in the morning, you said he would linger for days."

"He would have if it weren't for me," Gus replies sotto voce.

"What?" Maria asks in alarm. But before Gus can answer, the funeral director stands before them thrusting carnations into their hands. The casket has been lowered into the grave, and the mourners, one by one, pause to toss their flowers before returning to the limousines.

Gus opens the door of the first car and holds it for Vilma. He bends over to kiss her, but she turns abruptly away. Her dignified, but icy rejection is lost on everyone except Gus, who straightens up as if he had been slapped. Vilma slams the door harder than she should and diverts her focus to Anselm, who climbs in on the opposite side.

As the limousine pulls away, Gus remains motionless – in his eyes silent devastation, in his heart absolute loneliness.

Chapter Twenty-Five

Gus is sitting up in their antique canopied Queen Anne bed, his breakfast tray virtually untouched. His recollections have been revelations to Maria. She stands at the window, tears falling down her cheeks. How could she have missed the meaning of that scene? Why had she never asked Gus what had so shaken him that day? Why had she not probed for the cause of Gus' grief and anger? For the chill between him and Vilma? And why had she not connected the dots? Gus' birthday. . . Nils' death. . . the World Trade Towers. . . Gus' thoughts of suicide. . . that fateful coincidence of numbers!

Gus is spent after his long confessional. He buries his head in Rufus' fur, and the dog happily licks his human's face – great slobbery, forgiving kisses.

Wiping her eyes, Maria turns impulsively and walks toward the bed. She removes the breakfast trays, shoos Rufus down, and climbs into bed with Gus. With a shudder of relief, Gus reaches over and pulls Maria to him in a long, passionate kiss.

Sadly and gently, she disengages. "Gus, the doctor said – "

Gus silences her with his lips. She sits up.

"Ok," he groans in assent. He wraps Maria in the green paisley quilt and pulls her close to him. She snuggles into the curve of his arm and rests her head on his shoulder. His fingers trace the worry lines in her face, seeking to erase them. She closes her eyes and smiles.

Rufus yawns. "Nap time for all," he concurs.

✳✳✳

A few weeks later when the lush green of summer has erupted into the brilliant reds and oranges of fall, Gus and Maria, still in their robes, are sitting at the small table in their bedroom, sipping their morning coffee. They have almost finished their latest jigsaw puzzle: a whimsical gathering of cats in red hats.

"How do you feel today?" Maria queries.

"Great! I'm a new man!"

"It's a perfect day out there. Are you up for a walk? We can take Rufus on the trail."

"Sure, but let's finish the puzzle first."

"OK," Maria challenges. "I'll race you."

Giggling impishly, they begin grabbing pieces and thrusting them into place, each one trying to get the final piece.

"I'm going to beat you!" Gus crows.

"You're cheating!" Maria protests.

Just before Gus' hand closes over the last irregular cardboard chunk, Maria snatches it away from him. "I got it," she cries gleefully. She jumps into the bed and playfully hides the puzzle bit under the pillow.

Gus follows, pouncing on her, tickling her until she squeals, all the while trying to wrest the prize from Maria. Suddenly he abandons his pursuit of the puzzle. Gus looks searchingly at Maria and finds the answer he craves.

No objection this time as play gives way to lovemaking.

✳✳✳

Lovers now. Lovers always. The months following Gus' recovery from surgery pass in idyllic bliss. The demons of guilt, depression, worry have been, if not completely exorcised, then at least banished.

Gus and Maria rejoice in the NOW: the vivid fall foliage of the pristine woods; the tactile pleasure of soft pine needles underfoot as Rufus pads beside them on their daily walks; the breathtaking whiteness of those same woods after the first snowfall; a brilliant winter sun peeking through the tall pines adorned with heavy, wet snowflakes that shimmer like crystal; the stillness in the air enfolding the threesome as Rufus bounds through the drifts.

Maria laughs and claps her hands with childlike joy. Gus tosses a snowball for Rufus to retrieve before stooping down to make another to lob at Maria. Laughing gaily, she runs down the trail with Rufus in pursuit. When the bear-dog overtakes her, he puts his paws on her shoulders and knocks her over into the snow bank. He finishes his conquest by licking her face. So absorbed in frolic is Maria that she does not notice how winded Gus is by the time he catches up, nor does she see the slightly pained smile on her husband's face.

Chapter Twenty-Six

"At last, life is as it should be," Maria muses to herself on Christmas Eve as she and Gus are trimming their tree – one they had cut themselves earlier in the week. Rufus had helped them haul it from the farm, and Gus and Maria had proudly agreed that next winter they would have to add draft training to the dog's schedule.

Nostalgia engulfs Gus and Maria with each ornament they unwrap. So many symbols of the stages of their marriage: angels, musical instruments, cats, birds, moose, Newfs. Maria glances at their own peaceable kingdom: the great dog snoozing on the hearth and several Maine Coons snoring on the cat tree. As Gus adjusts the lights on the tree, Maria hangs the stockings on the mantle – one for Rufus and each cat and, of course, two larger ones for the humans. She starts arranging a huge assortment of wrapped boxes under the tree.

"Good heavens," Gus exclaims, "have we ever been shopping!"

"And, why not?" Maria counters. "Christmas is always my favorite holiday. And we have to give something to everyone in the family." She shakes a large package labeled "Rufus" to get the dog's attention. Sleepily, Rufus looks up and then, nonplussed, drops his head back onto his paws.

Gus slips *A Ceremony of Carols* into the CD player. He flips off the Tiffany chandelier and motions Maria to join him on the sofa. The bluish orange flames lick at the glass fireplace doors; the tree lights twinkle merrily as the boy soprano's plainsong rings out in dialogue with the harp.

Hodie. Christus natus est.

✳✳✳

"Should you?" Maria worries as Gus pops the cork on the well-chilled Veuve Clicquot to accompany their chocolate soufflé.

"It's a special celebration," Gus replies, pouring two flutes. The soft candlelight dances on the prismed crystal. Outside, thick cottony snowflakes stick noiselessly to the windowpanes.

"It has been a wonderful day," Maria concurs. "The best Christmas I have ever had! Just us." She pauses, and searching her husband's face for his reaction, she adds, "And the kids." At Gus' smile, Maria relaxes and beams at him.

"This should make it even better," Gus ventures, slipping a small blue box from his pocket and pushing it across the table toward Maria. She gasps when she sees the Cross Jewelers' ribbon. Hands trembling, she opens the box, knowing full well what it contains.

"Oh, my God, Gus, I thought we had said we'd wait for our fiftieth for this."

Reaching over to slip the "Lady Captain's Diamond" onto Maria's left hand, he whispers, "I may not be there for that one."

"Not true!" Maria exclaims, tears instantly welling up. "Not true," she repeats fiercely, picking up the plates and masking a hasty exit to the kitchen. She runs the faucet to cover her nose blow, composes herself, and returns to Gus. Bending over, she kisses him gently on the head.

Chapter Twenty-Seven

It is a crisp, sunny February Sunday. At Potts Point the sea and sky are sapphire, and snow glistens on the trees along the cottage-lined path to the beach.

Maria has hold of Rufus' leash and is struggling to keep up with him, so eager is the Newfoundland to get to the water. Gus has to stop several times to catch his breath. On the third pause, his hand flutters briefly to his chest.

"Hey, wait up!" he calls.

"I can't. He's pulling me." Maria disappears through the thicket and emerges on the strand. She finally corrals Rufus into a SIT and waits for Gus. Together they walk slowly toward the point.

"Are you OK, hon?"

"Yeah, I'm just out of breath."

"That's not good. You had better call the doctor tomorrow."

"I told him last week when I had my checkup. He said it was probably just the cold and not to let Rufus pull me."

"It's not all that cold today. Not for February." Gesturing toward a piece of driftwood, Maria suggests, "Why don't we sit down over there and let Rufus run a bit by himself?"

Gus unhooks Rufus' lead and tosses a stick for him to retrieve. Rufus bounds off toward the surf. Gus sits beside Maria, and they stare out at the crystalline water shimmering in the winter sun.

A loon swims gracefully in one of the inlets between the rocks. Suddenly, with an eerie cry, another loon swoops down to join its mate. Gus puts his arm around Maria. No need to speak. They simply soak in the majesty of the moment.

"It's my turn to say it," Gus reflects. "This IS Paradise!"

"They mate for life, you know," Maria observes wistfully, settling her head on Gus' shoulder in a contented silence. Staring out to sea, Maria allows herself to utter the long suppressed question: "Gus, can I ask you something?"

He, too, is riveted on the vast horizon. "Why did I think of leaving?"

Maria starts. He is reading her mind. She stammers apologetically. "No, I think I understand that one now. I was afraid of your demons, afraid I would lose everything that mattered to me – my job, the cats, you. And in my own fear, I didn't see that you were drowning, and I was helping to sink you."

Gus puts his finger on her lips. "Ssh.."

Undeterred, softly and deliberately, Maria frames the question. "Why did you stay?"

Gus touches her chin and turns her face toward him. "I think you know why." Her luminous hazel eyes tell him she does.

Breaking the mood, he whistles for Rufus. The dog comes loping back and drops the stick at their feet. Gus clips on the leash and appreciatively pats the big head.

"My turn to ask you something. If, for some reason, I can't do it, you'll make sure – promise me – that Rufus stays in water rescue training. He has too much talent to waste it. Even if he has to go live with Penny."

Maria does her best to disguise her alarm. "What made you think of that?"

"I don't know. Just being here, I guess." Gus gets up and takes a few steps with Rufus toward the incoming tide.

Wind in his hair, a flash of pain in those blue eyes searching the blue sea.

Chapter Twenty-Eight

Two days later, taking advantage of the still glorious winter weather, Gus has quit his desk a half hour earlier than usual in order to exercise on his treadmill. Facing the window, he can enjoy the last rays of daylight as the shadows lengthen through the snow-laden pines and the white birches confront the slate blue sky.

He flips on MSNBC, sets the controls on the machine, and checks his Blackberry one last time.

Maria pops her head into the doorway. "How long are you going to work out?"

"A half hour and then we can walk Rufus."

"OK, then I'll feed the cats and wait for you."

He nods and starts the treadmill. She closes the door and heads to the kitchen. As she fills cat bowls and sets them on trays, she checks the clock: 3:40 p.m.

✳✳✳

Gus is jogging at a good clip, his recently toned and lean body absorbed in the rhythm. He turns the volume down on the television and fills his lungs with air, taking in the stateliness of the woods – his woods – their woods.

Maria bustles back into the kitchen carrying the empty trays which she rinses and puts in the dishwasher. Checking the clock again – 4:02 p.m. – she is surprised by Rufus' whine.

"Rufus, where are you? Do you have to go out? Come on, I'll take you while Daddy finishes."

She rounds the corner from the kitchen into the hallway outside the exercise room. Whimpering, Rufus stands in front of the closed door. Seeing Maria, he barks and puts a paw on the handle. Maria takes his leash from the wall hook. She opens the door a crack and calls in above the whirr of the treadmill and the chatter of the TV.

"Gus, he has to pee. I'm going to walk him now."

No answer.

"Hon?" She pushes the door fully open. "Gus!" His name escapes her lips, a strangulated cry of anguish. In shock and to keep herself from fainting, she leans against the wall.

The machine is churning angrily, but Gus is not on it. He is lying face down on the floor. The Blackberry has fallen from his hand, and there are impact marks on the wall.

The long-denied, ever-present nightmare has become reality at last.

Chapter Twenty-Nine

Winter ambled into spring, and spring dazzled its way into summer. Maria neither saw nor felt the changes. Like a guillotine, a door had crashed down, bisecting here life – past cut off – future non-existant. She moved like a zombie through the endless procession of family and visitors in the weeks surrounding the funeral and cremation. Nights were sleepless. Days were filled with chores: settling Gus' affairs, assuring her own financial future, mechanically taking care of her furry friends and the home that had once been their castle, and learning to hire tradesmen or mowing the lawn herself. Food revolted her. The solitude terrified her. Her creative muse had deserted her. She could not write; she could not express in words, which had always been her solace and her gift, the terrible nausea which held her in its grip, the vast emptiness which engulfed her.

She hit bottom. For the first time in her life, she knew the agony with which Gus had lived; she faced the all-consuming demon of depression. Old friends were lifelines, but one June day she realized she could not battle alone.

She sought and found an ally in Daniel Whitman, a therapist whose compassion, empathy, intelligence, and gentleness offered the rescue net she needed so desperately. She poured out the twists and turns of her story – their story – to Daniel. She wept; she hurled recriminations at herself; she reached out into memory seeking the whys of Gus and her history. In her search to forgive and be forgiven, she examined every moment of their lives together; she reconstructed the architecture of a love that for forty years had been the *raison d'être* of her very existence. She chided herself for her mistakes, her insensitivities, her obtuseness at certain junctures of their lives. Gus' hurtfulness she erased; in a heartbeat she would do every minute of every day of their marriage over again. He had been, for better or for worse, her soul mate, and the connection they had shared remained ever present and indestructible.

And when she planned Gus' memorial for late summer, she created a ceremony that paid tribute – not to all his accomplishments as a man – but to the uniqueness of their love and to the poignancy of their now shattered dream.

✳✳✳

The sun burns like a beacon through the majestic pine trees on the August day. It holds for Maria the warmth of Gus' smile. The lawns are mulched and manicured. Their gardens are in full bloom. The centerpiece is a memory bench on which Maria has had inscribed *And if God choose, I shall but love thee better after death – Elizabeth Barrett Browning.* Behind the bench a copper sculpture of a blue heron, their favorite bird, stands, a mysterious and inchoate guardian. Beneath the white tent facing the woods, fifty of their friends and family are assembled.

The bagpipes wail the *Highland Lament,* a call to remembrance. Poems are read; folk songs and hymns are played; spontaneous reminiscences are shared in the Quaker fashion before Maria, wearing a flowing white eyelet skirt and sleeveless white sweater, steps to the podium to offer her farewell.

She thanks her friends and neighbors. She tells of the dreams she and Gus have shared and of their brief Maine idyll. She talks of the sea and tells the story of the pair of loons at Potts Point. She recalls that

> *Thoreau was Greg's favorite writer. He loved <u>The Maine Woods</u> the best, and, of course, we both loved <u>Walden</u>, and it is in <u>Walden</u> that Thoreau writes:*
>
> *'I came to the woods because I wished to live deliberately, to front only the essential facts of life, and see if I could not learn what it had to teach, and not, when it came time to die, discover that I had not lived.'*
>
> *Greg did, indeed, live a very full and rich life for sixty-three-and-a-half*

years, the last year of which was uniquely satisfying to him. And, so, I would like to think that when it did come time to die on that treadmill at just before 4:00 p.m. on Feb. 23 of this year, that the last thing he saw was these woods. I like to believe that in that instant between the vibrancy of the present and the silence of eternity, there was a comforting epiphany: his life had embraced the essentials, that he had lived well, and that his dream had been, however briefly, realized.

Then, her last words segue seamlessly into the piper's song, *Amazing Grace, how sweet thou art.*

✳✳✳

The notes hum in Maria's head. Anselm drives her van, leading a cortege to Potts Point. The mourners reassemble behind the piper, who leads them down the dirt road. *Where have all the flowers gone? Long time passing* intone the pipes piteously.

Maria leans on Anselm's arm; she carries a basket with Gus' urn smothered over in pink carnations. The procession passes through the copse. Ingrid, Helmi, Betsy, and Peter follow with Rufus trudging beside Peter on lead. They reach the beach. Tide is high, and only a narrow sandbar separates Middle Bay from Harpswell Sound.

The piper stops at the designated spot not far out onto the embankment. He sounds the last hymn: *We Shall Overcome.* The bereaved assemble in a row behind the piper. Rufus sits obediently, riveting his gaze on the sea.

As the last verse finishes – *We shall not forget* – Maria tucks up her skirt and wades out into the water; Anselm carries the urn.

"Do you want to say something?" Anselm asks gently.

Maria chokes back her tears and stammers, "Goodbye, my love. Be at peace. I love you always."

Anselm unscrews the cork and, swinging his arms like a pendulum, slowly scatters Gus' ashes. Swirling around them, the water colors pinkish grey as the remains float languidly. Impulsively, Maria dips her hand into the brine and touches it to her lips, a last kiss. Then, wheeling around, she wades back to the beach, followed by Anselm. Betsy has distributed the carnations among the mourners. She hands the last two to her husband and Maria. One by one, the family files to the water's edge, and each tosses a flower into the tide.

Maria's lips move silently, as if in prayer. *How do I love thee? Let me count the ways.* As she finishes, *I love thee with the breath, smiles, tears of all my life – And if God choose, I shall but love thee better after death.* With that vow she flings her carnation and steps back, weeping silently. Anselm puts his arm around her shoulder.

All eyes are trained on the ashes and flowers, which advance and recede, floating lyrically in the swell. Slowly, some flowers are pulled out to sea with the receding tide, but two intertwine and persistently refuse to drift away. Back and forth, caressed by the ashes, they are buoyed toward the shore and then toward the horizon. A hush falls over the company. Their farewell has been echoed and answered. All of a sudden, Rufus stirs and pulls fiercely on the lead, trying to enter the water where his beloved Gus' remains linger. Peter restrains him. Maria drops to her knees. To console and be consoled, she buries her face on Rufus' neck, sobbing.

Chapter Thirty

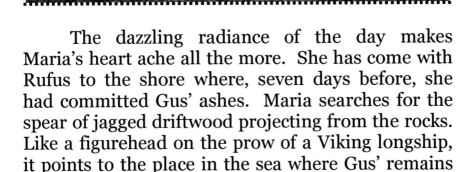

The dazzling radiance of the day makes Maria's heart ache all the more. She has come with Rufus to the shore where, seven days before, she had committed Gus' ashes. Maria searches for the spear of jagged driftwood projecting from the rocks. Like a figurehead on the prow of a Viking longship, it points to the place in the sea where Gus' remains began their long journey into infinity.

Maria sits on a nearby log, looking fixedly at the water. A lobster boat putters far off shore, and loons and gulls paddle contentedly in the inlets. The cobalt sea is luminous and secretive – not a trace.

"Gus, oh my Gus, where are you now? I love you so much." She shields her eyes into the sun and catches sight of Rufus, who is wading in the shallows. Suddenly, he picks up something from the sand and bounds back to Maria. Putting his head in her lap, he deposits two pink carnations entangled with seaweed.

"Oh, Gus, you are here! You'll always be!" She hugs Rufus, grabs a stick, and tosses it. The dog gleefully scurries into the water to retrieve.

Alone on the sand, tears stream down Maria's cheeks, falling in rivulets on the upturned corners of her smile.

"Gus, Rufus," she murmurs.

⁂

Once home, Maria heads directly to the phone.

"Penny, it's Maria."

"How are you holding up, hon?" her friend asks.

"Barely," Maria admits as she steadies herself by sitting at the little roll-top kitchen desk. "I went to Potts Point today. I go to talk him, you know? And Rufus found two carnations from last week's ceremony. They had been out to sea and back. Watching Rufus splash in those waves, I remembered what I had promised Gus last winter. I don't want Rufus to miss the rest of the training sessions. I know you'll take good care of him."

As she is confiding to Penny, Skrimshander ambles into the kitchen and, sensing her need of comfort, jumps into her lap and begins to knead.

"I will," Penny tells her gently. "Are you ready? John and I can come get him tomorrow."

"No, not really," a little girl voice replies. "But, yeah. Yeah, come."

Maria hangs up the phone without another word and wipes her eyes. Skrimshander reaches his muzzle up and offers the consolation of a head butt.

Chapter Thirty-One

A crisp, clear, warm Indian summer morning on deserted Popham Beach. Maria barefoot with jeans rolled up walks languidly along the shoreline, her eyes searching the sand, judging her distance by the vanishing sandbar. At last, she determines the exact spot and focuses on the sea for a very long time. Then she kneels down and uses her finger to trace a message on the smooth, blank slate of sand.

Slowly, she draws a large heart and scrawls *forever love*. Next she outlines two smaller hearts and connects all three with a single arrow. Then, she adds the names: in one *Gus* and in the other *Maria*. She stands to survey her valentine.

Shielding her eyes against the luminous autumn sun, she scans the horizon. So bright is the light that for an instant she is blinded. In the shimmering white expanse, Gus wading in the surf with Rufus. His eyes sapphire as the sea, the corners of his bow-shaped lips flicked upward in an enigmatic smile.

A frisson of energy courses through her body. She shivers and blinks. Nothing. Nothing now –

Maria smiles thoughtfully, squats down, and adds to her drawing a third heart and arrow. Inside this one she writes *Rufus*. Then beneath the entire hieroglyphic she adds the date: *9/11/2010*.

Rising slowly to her feet, she again pans the horizon hoping for another revelation. Only sun, sand, and water. The lapping waves creep closer and closer to the writing at her feet.

Maria wipes away a single tear.

The water steals forward to erase her words – first *Rufus*. Then *Maria*. She cannot watch. She smiles sadly and turns to walk back up the beach.

She is a dark, distant speck when the cool brine gently obliterates Gus' name.

Again, only sun, sand, and sea. The slate is once more blank.

Postlude

Rippling water and endless sky. An advancing ribbon of undulating cerulean washes over the opalescent sands. Like the Leviathan, the sandbar sinks slowly into the deep. Only the intermittent and rhythmic flash of Seguin's beacon.

✳✳✳

Vast, still water. The lilac grey morning light. Mighty Kathadin, a silent sentinel above the opposite shore. A blonde woman tosses a life preserver into the lake. A giant bear-dog makes a *grande jeté* into the water and swims to retrieve. A *pas de deux*, Penny and Rufus practice the Newfoundland's ancient ritual.

✳✳✳

Where the jagged driftwood spear points to the open sea, the widow sits on the sand, pockmarked by shells and pebbles. Between her knees, she cradles a large black ball of fur. The ten-week-old puppy enthusiastically licks the woman's face. Gently, Maria Sundergaard redirects the Newfie's attention toward Harpswell Sound. Transfixed, she rests her chin on the dog's head and whispers into the floppy ear.

"There, Ruffian, look!"

In the watery inlet between the crags paddle a pair of loons.

About the Author

Born and raised in the metropolitan New York area, Carla Maria Verdino-Süllwold took her degrees at Sarah Lawrence College and Fairleigh Dickinson University. She began her career as a teacher and arts administrator before becoming a journalist, critic, and author. Her music and visual arts reviews and features appeared regularly in *Opera News, Gramophone, Opéra International, Opera, Music Magazine, Beaux Arts*, and *The Crisis*, and her byline headed numerous program essays and record liner notes. Among her scholarly works, the best known is *We Need A Hero! Heldentenors from Wagner's Time to the Present: A Critical History.* She helped to create several television projects, serving as associate producer and content consultant/writer, among them *I Hear America Singing* for WNET/PBS and *Voices of the Heart: Stephen Foster* for German television. She is also the author of *Top Cat Tails of Mannahatta*, a fictional account of her and husband Gregory's adventures in breeding Maine Coons.

In 2009 the Süllwolds realized a lifelong dream to move to coastal Maine. *Raising Rufus A Maine Love Story* is a fictionalized account of the couple's last year together with their beloved Newfoundland, Rufus, before Gregory Süllwold's fatal heart attack in February 2010.

Now semi-retired, Ms. Verdino-Süllwold continues to write and teach part time. She shares her home in Brunswick, Maine, with her kitties and a new Newfoundland puppy, Ruffian.

CPSIA information can be obtained at www.ICGtesting.com
Printed in the USA
BVOW011127221011

274211BV00005B/4/P

9 781450 784634